Iris van Herpen

FASHION AUTEURS

Series Editors

Adam Geczy and Vicki Karaminas

Fashion Auteurs is a groundbreaking book series devoted to designers who have left an indelible mark on fashion history. Critical, clear and concise, each title, comprising around 30K words, is written by authorities in the field, situating each designer within their time and against their peers, with a focus on the contributions that have made them memorable. Using the term 'auteur' to designate film directors with a distinctive and influential style, this is the first series to treat fashion designers and related fashion creators (e.g. photographers) as on par with artists who have decisively shaped imagery, taste, and what is seen to be current and desirable. These books will be of interest not only to fashionistas and ardent devotees of fashion magazines but also to students and teachers of art and design, artists and designers themselves, not to mention anyone seeking a deeper acquaintance with fashion and design culture.

Forthcoming Titles in the Series

Adam Geczy, *Rose Bertin*
Vanessa Gerrie, *Manfred Thierry Mugler*
Scott Wilson, *Anton Corbijn*
Simona Segre-Reinach, *Romeo Gigli*
Patrizia Calefato, *Franco Moschino*
Nicola Brajato, *Walter Van Beirendonck*
Alexander Zamboni, *Robert Cavalli*

Iris van Herpen

Anneke Smelik

ANTHEM PRESS

Anthem Press
An imprint of Wimbledon Publishing Company
www.anthempress.com

This edition first published in UK and USA 2027
by ANTHEM PRESS
75–76 Blackfriars Road, London SE1 8HA, UK
or PO Box 9779, London SW19 7ZG, UK
and
244 Madison Ave #116, New York, NY 10016, USA

British Library Cataloguing-in-Publication Data
A catalogue record for this book is available from the British Library.

Library of Congress Cataloging-in-Publication Data: 2026943002

ISBN-13: 978-1-80136-116-3 (Hbk) / 978-1-80136-117-0 (Pbk)
ISBN-10: 1-80136-116-9 (Hbk) / 1-80136-117-7 (Pbk)

This title is also available as an eBook.

CONTENTS

LIST OF FIGURES

ACKNOWLEDGEMENTS

The research for Maison *Iris van Herpen* has unfolded over the past 10 years, and I am indebted to the many colleagues and friends who accompanied me along this journey. Daniëlle Bruggeman and Lianne Toussaint have been wonderful fellow travellers in our shared fashion research. I am especially grateful to fashion curator Ninke Bloemberg of the Centraal Museum, who showed me Iris van Herpen's dresses in the museum archive in 2018.

In 2019, I visited Atelier Iris van Herpen in Amsterdam and interviewed Head of the Atelier Petra Schuddeboom and then commercial director Paul van As. Both generously shared a wealth of information about the workings of the studio and offered valuable insight into the design process. Unfortunately, the Atelier was unable to accommodate a second visit in 2026, but members of the team kindly answered several of my questions by email. I would particularly like to thank Kecia Benvenuto, Head of Partnerships, Collaborations & PR, for her patience with my continuous stream of emails, and Social Media & PR Manager Joshua Lockley for helping to locate the images for this book. My sincere thanks go to the series editors Adam Geczy and Vicky Karaminas for welcoming this book into their series and for their incisive feedback on the first draft. I am grateful to my lifelong friend Bernadette van Dijck for being such an attentive and thoughtful reader of the manuscript. Finally, I thank Rosi Braidotti for being a constant source of inspiration throughout my intellectual journey and our life together.

INTRODUCTION

Iris van Herpen: An Introduction

Is it fashion? Is it art? Is it technology? Can it be worn as a garment? How is it even made? Iris van Herpen's experimental designs raise such questions. The easy answer is that Iris van Herpen's innovative designs are a mix – she merges fashion with art, science, technology and the natural environment. Avant-garde, futuristic, innovative, cutting edge: these are the words that are often used to describe Iris van Herpen's fashion designs. Her aesthetic style is successful, considering how many stars and celebrities wear her designs. To name just a few: Björk, Lady Gaga, Rihanna, Beyoncé and Ariana Grande for their concerts and album covers; Naomi Campbell, Cara Delevingne and Cate Blanchett for the red carpet, and the Dutch Queen Máxima for her 50th birthday party in 2021.

Figure I.1 Portrait of Iris van Herpen, 2022. © Photographer Robin de Puy.

Dutch fashion designer Iris van Herpen (1984) rose to fame with her first 3D-printed pieces from the collection 'Crystallization' in 2010 (see Figure 1.2). Rapid prototyping enabled van Herpen to materialise digital designs with a 3D printer, producing elaborate folds without the need for needle and thread. The intricacy of the three-dimensional folds allowed by the then-new technology of 3D printing was quite unique (see Figures 1.3 and 2.1). 3D design and printing has brought about a revolution in design practice, opening up possibilities of creating new forms that would have been impossible when designing by hand on a flat sheet. 'In everything I do, I need to push the boundaries', she says.[1]

Iris van Herpen matches the experimental and innovative structure of her work with equal creativity and freedom of expression in her language. She often invents new and rather peculiar words for her collections, which read like lyrics of songs: 'Syntopia', 'Biopiracy' or 'Architectonics'. She also creates titles of two words that indicate paradox, ambiguity or an oxymoronic expression, like 'Wilderness Embodied', 'Hybrid Holism', 'Radiation Invasion', 'Refinery Smoke' or 'Chemical Crows' or 'Earthrise'. Or she uses Japanese expressions like 'Seijaku', or Latin, like 'Ludi Naturae' or 'Quaquaversal' or Greek, like 'Sympoiesis'. Such neologisms refer to one of Iris van Herpen's defining characteristics, which is working with apparent contradictions and flaring incongruities. 'Seijaku', for example, is a Japanese aesthetic of seeking tranquillity in the midst of activity, while 'quaquaversal' means going off in all directions from the centre. By literally coining new words and expressions for the titles of her collections, Iris van Herpen invents a new language for her designs. At the same time, the surrealist aesthetics of her designs create a new visual and material language.

Accelerating the synergies between fashion, art, science and technology, van Herpen always looks for collaborations: with artists, musicians, architects, scientists. She even worked with the world-class Swiss/European scientific research facility CERN. Another source of inspiration is what we have learned to call nature: van Herpen's designs merge the artificial with the organic, performing biomimicry in shaping dresses like spider webs, coral reefs, the rhizomic roots of fungi, undulating waves of water or smoke, marine organisms or the dendrites and synapses of neural networks. Recently, van Herpen has ventured into sculptural art; monumental yet ethereal textile installations made of tulle, silk and 3D-printed elements (see Figure C.1). Even beyond the nature–culture continuum, van Herpen designs a material universe of its own, which is neither post-natural nor post-technological but new 'otherwise', new in a radically 'other' way.

Yet, significantly, sartorial craftsmanship remains important to van Herpen's approach to cutting-edge technologies. Each garment, however much technologically designed and manufactured, is finished with the finest detail by hand. Like a true digital artisan, she is always searching for a way to fill the gap between the computer process and the traditional craftsmanship that is done by hand. As Iris van Herpen comments:

> The combination of craftsmanship and new technology is crucial for me, because it gives a tension between the possibilities of technology and the redundancy of traditional techniques. I do not want to resolve this tension by only designing clothes in a high-tech way, but I sustain the tension by giving ample space to manual workmanship.[2]

For her, science, technology and craftsmanship should come together into a fusion where they can enhance one another. Manual labour, abstract concepts and technological know-how converge in a practice that breaks down boundaries and points in new directions. This focus on craftsmanship is van Herpen's response to the intimate connection we are nurturing towards the technological world we live in; she shows that craftsmanship and technology, far from excluding one another, actually go hand in hand. This insight harks back to the original meaning of the Greek word *tékhnē*: art, skill, craft. The focus on manual craftsmanship expresses an interest in the raw materiality of matter in a hi-tech world of mediated virtual technologies. The artisanal qualities that are imbibed in craftsmanship bring the technologies within the grip of our hands, making the hi-tech world more human and accessible.

While van Herpen engages hands-on with the materiality of textiles and textures, as a fashion designer she is also acutely aware of and interested in the materiality of the human skin and body. The futuristic designs have a consequence for the way in which the human – mostly female – body comes to be represented in her work. A techno-optimist, Iris van Herpen experiments with the ways in which we can shape our bodies or perform our identities, not in a flight away from the flesh, but rather by plunging deeper into it. Her designs create hybrid forms of the human body, but they do so by merging humans with animals, trees or plants, wisps of smoke, magnets, sound waves or dendrites and synapses. There is a sort of natural enhancement at play in her work, which the technologies intensify, but do not produce alone. Van Herpen's designs denaturalise the human body, but also bring it closer to a contemporary natural order, which is always already mediated. The bodies thus designed are weird in the mode of the fantastic: inside-out, with lumps and bumps in odd places, shrouded in a splash of water or a cloud of smoke, covered in 3D-printed spikes, snowflakes or eerie feathers, or cloaked in circular shapes and geometric patterns made of silicone, polyamide, metal or glass. This is the most radical impact of her futuristic aesthetic: the alienating and haunting denaturalisation of the human figure through technological mediation and new materials. But they also cleverly point in the direction of animals, plants, rocks and climatic elements. In either case, such visionary designs move us out of the comfort zone of our wardrobes, opening up a horizon beyond conventional fashion. Van Herpen's fashion designs confuse boundaries between human and hi-tech, or human and animal, and shift ambiguous borders between skin and textile, organic and technological, material and digital. The message is that the human is deeply entangled with the wider material world, both organically and technologically, and that, far from being a catastrophe, such hybrid interconnectedness is a rich source of inspiration for new modes of relation to others.

Iris van Herpen asks us to engage affectively with the fusion of fashion, art, nature and technology. Already early in her career she said: 'I just do not subscribe to the slogan 'Form follows function.' Instead, I look for shapes that complement and change the body and thus the emotion. Movement, so essential to and in the body, is just as important in my work.'[3] In a way, she believes that 'form follows emotion'. Iris van Herpen wonders: 'Can emotions be materialised? I believe it is possible to merge, move and stir our sense through a sensitive balance of textures, shapes and colors.'[4] Considering the enormous success of the exhibition *Sculpting the Senses* that toured from 2023 to 2026, from Paris, to Singapore, to Brisbane, to Rotterdam and to New York, people are indeed moved and affected by these futuristic fashion designs. The latest news is that the exhibition will also tour to Korea, Japan and China.

Maison Iris van Herpen does not follow the seasons nor does it set fashion trends; in the strict sense of the word, the designs are not commercially fashionable. Her collaborative and process-driven approach to fashion practice means that she privileges process over product and artistic design over normative business. Rather, her designs are forward-looking. The innovative dresses are 'one of the present day's most visionary expressions of technology'.[5] And in pointing to a future in which fashion, art, science and technology are realised in a synthesis, they capture the potential spirit of creation of today. A spirit that understands that only in this mix can we express awe of nature, familiarity with technological culture as well as the desire for sustainability.

In this book, I argue that interpreting Iris van Herpen's designs requires new methods of analysis and fresh theoretical frameworks. Her work resists conventional approaches to cultural inquiry and fashion analysis; it simply cannot be fully understood within their limits. When I began researching van Herpen's designs about a decade ago, I found myself both inspired and challenged as a fashion scholar. Her work prompted me to develop a new methodology – new materialism – and to engage with posthumanism as a theoretical framework for fashion studies. This book therefore grounds its interpretation of van Herpen's highly technological designs within these two perspectives.

In the chapters that follow, I demonstrate how Iris van Herpen creates a distinctly contemporary aesthetic. Her pioneering designs stage encounters between craftsmanship and technology, the organic and the inorganic and between art, science and nature. I describe this aesthetic as 'posthuman' because it emerges from these hybrid interactions – between sartorial tradition and cutting-edge innovation, materiality and immateriality. Van Herpen dresses a posthuman body: one that is environmentally situated yet permeated by technology and new materials. Her fashion moves fluidly between categories, occupying the space between human and non-human. This is characteristic of posthumanism, which conceives of life as dynamic and entangled, with human bodies inseparable from fibres, fabrics, garments and technologies. Vibrant and alive, van Herpen's designs foreground the interdependence of humans, nature and technology. Through a rich vocabulary of ripples, loops, folds, waves, twists, pleats, wrinkles and circles, her baroque forms explore the vitality of matter, form and time. This book shows how her sculptural designs invite us to understand life as an ongoing process of transformation and metamorphosis.

The first chapter offers a comprehensive overview of Iris van Herpen's career and the workings of her Amsterdam-based atelier. I examine the intricate design processes within the studio, highlighting the synergy between advanced technologies and meticulous handicraft. This process is inherently dynamic, shifting with each new project. The chapter demonstrates how this hybrid approach – combining digital innovation with artisanal practice – creates a fertile ground for pushing the boundaries of contemporary fashion.

The second chapter focuses on van Herpen's pioneering use of 3D printing, which propelled her to international recognition as one of fashion's leading innovators. I outline the technologies behind 3D printing and their role in shaping some of her most groundbreaking designs. To situate these innovations, I introduce the frameworks of new materialism and posthumanism, which together illuminate her work as a dynamic negotiation between human and non-human realms. From this perspective, van Herpen's designs can be understood as enacting a posthuman aesthetic – a continuum between nature and culture, biology and technology.

In the third chapter, I turn to one of the most persistent motifs in van Herpen's oeuvre: the exuberant fold. Drawing on Gilles Deleuze's concept of the fold, I explore its multiple meanings and implications. The fold is inherently expressive; its movements suggest expansion, opening the subject to a process of becoming that is never fixed. Through the fold, van Herpen articulates transformation as continuous – garment and wearer alike fold, enfold, unfold and refold, embodying an ongoing metamorphosis.

The fourth chapter examines one of van Herpen's central sources of inspiration: nature. Her designs engage with phenomena such as water, smoke, mycelium and the delicate movement of bird wings, spanning both microcosmic and cosmic scales. This expansive vision of nature also informs her commitment to sustainability. At the heart of the chapter is the 'living dress', composed of 125 million bioluminescent algae that emit light in response to movement. When not worn, the garment is preserved in a controlled glass environment to sustain the life of the algae. This remarkable piece encapsulates van Herpen's approach to design – one that integrates living systems into fashion, redefining the relationship between garment and life.

The fifth chapter explores van Herpen's engagement with the human body and movement, shaped by her background in classical ballet and modern dance. Movement is central to her design philosophy, and she has created costumes for dance, opera and theatre. Designing for performance introduces challenges of durability, visibility and flexibility. Her collaborations with choreographers have produced visually striking yet sometimes restrictive garments, such as heavy dresses or tightly fitted leather suits. These works reveal a tension between artistic experimentation and functional performance. In later projects, however, van Herpen moves towards feathery and flowing dresses, purposefully exploring a fluid and flexible identity.

Finally, the conclusion returns to the posthuman aesthetic that defines Iris van Herpen's work, drawing together the threads of transformation, hybridity and becoming that run throughout the book.

Notes

1 Quoted in Hans Ulrich Obrist, 'Interview with Iris van Herpen' in Catalogue *Iris van Herpen: Sculpting the Senses.* (Amsterdam: Lannoo, 2023), 29.

2 Quoted in Ninke Bloemberg (ed.), *Het Nieuwe Ambacht: Iris van Herpen en haar inspiratie* ['The New Craft: Iris van Herpen and Her Inspiration']. (Utrecht: Centraal Museum, 2011), 11, my translation.
3 Ibid.
4 Iris van Herpen, Catalogue *Iris van Herpen: Sculpting the Senses*. (Amsterdam: Lannoo, 2023), 35.
5 Bradley Quinn, *Fashion Futures*. (London: Merrell, 2012), 12.

Chapter 1

THE MAISON OF IRIS VAN HERPEN

Iris van Herpen was born on 5 June 1984, in the small village of Wamel in the Netherlands.[1] Wamel lies between two large rivers that shape much of the flat Dutch landscape. Perhaps the softly flowing water of those wide rivers has inspired the sense of fluidity that can be found in so many of her designs. Another source of childhood inspiration was her training in classical and modern dance, which made her forever aware of the movements and potentials of the body. Iris van Herpen says:

> If I were to use one word to describe my work, it would be movement, as one of the most influential things in my life has been my classical ballet practice. Through dance I learned about the seduction of movement, the transformation of the body, and the evolution of shape. Those years taught me how to shift shape and were the birth of my interest in fashion.[2]

She also had violin and painting lessons from a young age. She developed a first fascination for fashion when, as a child, she discovered old garments and costumes in her grandmother's attic. Deciding to study fashion rather than dance, Iris van Herpen moved to Arnhem to follow Fashion Design at ArtEZ Institute of the Arts, graduating in 2006. During her studies, she fulfilled internships in 2005 with Alexander McQueen in London and with textile designer Claudy Jongstra in Amsterdam.

This chapter traces an overview of Iris van Herpen's career and the operations of her Amsterdam-based atelier. It explores the studio's complex design methods, emphasising the interplay between cutting-edge technologies and painstaking craftsmanship. These methods remain fluid, evolving from one project to the next. I argue that this fusion of digital and technological experimentation and artisanal techniques provides a productive framework for expanding the possibilities of contemporary fashion.

Iris van Herpen started her label and studio in 2007, launching haute couture collections of highly technological designs under the cryptic logo | v | - | which is a visual rendition of her initials: I.v.H (see Figure 1.1). Ever since, van Herpen has maintained a consistent collection schedule, created in her atelier on the first floor of an old warehouse in Amsterdam, overlooking harbours and the water of the river IJ (yes, it's a strange name) that separates the inner city of Amsterdam from its northern parts and opens up on the IJ-lake (formerly an inner sea). Her studio

IRIS VAN HERPEN

Figure 1.1 The elegant yet cryptic logo. © Maison Iris van Herpen.

then sits in-between; in between earth, water and air: neither in the city nor in the countryside.

She presents her very first collection 'Fragile Futurity' at the Amsterdam Fashion Week in 2007. Her next collections are presented at the Amsterdam Fashion Week (2007–10) and some pieces also at the London Fashion Week (2009 and 2010): 'Refinery Smoke', 2008; 'Chemical Crows', 2008; 'Mummification', 2009; 'Radiation Invasion', 2009; 'Synesthesia', 2010; and 'Crystallization', 2010. She immediately makes an impression in the field of fashion with her innovative and experimental designs. All of those collections, which are no longer shown on her website, already showcase so many of her stylistic, rather baroque, features: intricate folds, the use of technology and her aesthetics of catching ephemeral phenomena, like smoke, water, the flight of a bird or a sound wave, in tangible forms.[3]

The year 2010 marks a turning point in her early career: Iris van Herpen presents her first 3D-printed piece from the collection called 'Crystallization': the famous white top that features on the cover of the catalogue of her big retrospective *Sculpting the Senses* (2023) (see Figure 1.2). It is an instant success and makes her recognised as one of the most innovative

Figure 1.2 Iris van Herpen, collection 'Crystallization', A/W 2010, as shown at the exhibition *Sculpting the Senses* (Paris, 2023). 3D-printed white polyamide top, made in collaboration with architect Daniel Widrig. © Photo Anneke Smelik.

fashion designers of today. It is inspired by shell structures and 3D-printed from white polyamide.

By 2011, she becomes the youngest guest member invited by the *Chambre Syndicale de la Haute Couture* (the Trade Association of High Fashion) in Paris to show her collections twice a year at Paris Fashion Week, which she does until 2024. In that year she decides to reduce the number of collections to one per year. Iris van Herpen makes her debut in Paris with the collection 'Capriole' (French for 'a leap in the air', 2011), which shows a compilation of highlights from previous collections, but also presents five new outfits that 'evoke the feeling just before and during a free-fall parachute jump'.[4] It is well known that Iris van Herpen is a keen parachute jumper since the age of 17, and the 'Capriole' collection embodies all the various emotions she experiences during falling.[5]

Maison Iris van Herpen almost exclusively designs haute couture. She produced a ready-to-wear collection only for a few years: Autumn/Winter 2013 to Spring/Summer 2016. In 2015, the ready-to-wear collection was made together with the couture collection 'Magnetic Motion' but usually the ready-to-wear collections were shown at the Women's Fair during Fashion Week in Paris. There is a whole system behind ready-to-wear that van Herpen feels uncomfortable about, but the biggest problem that she has with ready-to-wear is the fit: 'I began with couture, and I love to make a piece that fits the body perfectly.'[6] In 2016, Iris van Herpen decided to solely dedicate her time to haute couture because she felt that ready-to-wear presented her with too many restrictions for her way of designing.[7]

For the haute couture collections, van Herpen experiences the pressure and the deadline of the bi-annual winter and summer seasons as something positive, because without limitations in time, the process of endless development would never stop. Just like the body brings a certain demarcation for the design, so does the restriction in time. Neither the cycle of seasons nor fashion trends are particularly relevant for the collections, because 'the designs are more a marriage of art and fashion'.[8] Her first collections may have quirky names, but they were not yet labelled Autumn/Winter or Spring/Summer; this only is added when van Herpen begins showing her collections in Paris, starting with 'Capriole' (A/W 2011).

Since its founding year, 2007, the Maison of Iris van Herpen has been pushing an interdisciplinary dialogue between fashion, art, science and technology. As Vanessa Gerrie writes, 'Van Herpen acts as a creative director, researcher, curator, and practitioner for her brand. Her borderless fashion practice integrates brand image, technical innovation, and visual storytelling. These three elements intersect to curate a design identity.'[9] She has worked particularly with the art disciplines of dance and architecture, as I will further explore in Chapter 5. Curator Cloé Pitiot writes, 'Since 2007, Iris van Herpen's creations have been disrupting the codes of fashion and opening doors to universes seemingly unrelated to her disciplines. Her insatiable curiosity leads her to explore distant domains, drawing inspiration from contemporary art, architecture, the life sciences, art history, alchemy and mysticism alike.'[10] Merging different disciplines makes up an important part of her creative process, which I described in the Introduction as hybrid encounters between traditional craftsmanship, environmental grounding and future-facing technology. Within the Dutch field of design, her baroque style is considered rather 'un-Dutch'.[11] Dutch design is known for its straight lines and functionalism, still adhering to the 'form follows function' motto of early nineteenth-century modernism. But it is perhaps better to consider Iris van Herpen as someone who would rather believe in the motto 'form follows feeling'.[12]

Morphing fashion, art and technology, van Herpen develops cross-sectoral collaborations throughout her career with scientists, architects, artists, choreographers, filmmakers, hat makers, graphic designers, jewellery designers, musicians and so on. Multiple other practices consequently come to bear on her own designs. To innovate, she researches the effects of different materials and enters into interdisciplinary collaborations for the design of her collections. Such collaborations are usually based on mutual inspiration. Some partnerships are enduring, like with Icelandic singer Björk, Showstudio of British photographer Nick Knight and especially the 'living architecture' studio of Canadian architect Philip Beesley. Also for the practical production of materials, prints and dyes, she looks for collaborations with other – often commercial – partners; the Maison is always on the lookout for people who want to innovate.[13] Curator Louise Curtis writes that for Iris van Herpen fashion is 'a genuine vector of research, inquiry and experimentation. [...] By means of the vast network of interconnections between domains that constitute the essence of her unifying and comprehensive view, she envisions her collaborations as an awakening to infinite possibilities.'[14]

It is clear that Maison Iris van Herpen works outside the conventional business structures, which raises the question of how the relatively small fashion house remains financially viable. After all, she does not produce for ready-to-wear nor for mass production. The Maison regularly receives public funds, subsidies or awards, but the revenues also derive from sales of designs to museums, collectors and couture clients. The website systematically shows all the stars and celebrities who wear a mostly borrowed, sometimes bought, design on the red carpet, which enhances the glamorous look that Maison Iris van Herpen has boasted in the last few years.[15]

From the early beginning of her career, Iris van Herpen received several awards for her designs, starting with the Dutch Design Award twice, both in 2009 and 2010. To name just a few honours: Within her home country, the Netherlands, she was appointed a member of the respected Royal Academy of the Arts in 2015 (Akademie van Kunsten), and she was awarded the prestigious Johannes Vermeer Prize for best artist of the year in 2017. The list is too long to mention here, but internationally she was named 'Chevalier des Arts et des Lettres' in 2023, one of France's highest cultural honours. In 2025, she was awarded the 'Oscar' for fashion: the Fashion Visionary Award at the Fashion Group International's Annual Night of Stars Gala in New York City. And in 2026, Iris van Herpen was announced as the winner of the inaugural Perrier-Jouët Design for Nature

Award. The prize spotlights designers pushing sustainability in bold and creative ways, through the spirit of Art Nouveau – a philosophy that celebrates the interconnectedness of nature, culture and creativity. The prize involves a commission to design a new work for Design Miami 2026. The many awards and honours confirm van Herpen's influential position in the international design world.

The Centraal Museum in Utrecht and the Groninger Museum in Groningen, both in the Netherlands, were the first museums lucky enough to buy van Herpen's early designs. Lucky–because by now the designs are too expensive for these museums to acquire. Her fashion designs have been bought by world-leading museums, including the Metropolitan Museum of Art in New York, the Victoria and Albert Museum in London, the National Gallery of Victoria in Melbourne and the Palais de Tokyo in Paris.

Another sign of van Herpen's position in the field of fashion design is the high number of exhibitions dedicated to her work. In 2011, the exhibition *The New Craft* at the Centraal Museum Utrecht focused on the experimental work of Iris van Herpen and her sources of inspiration (Figure 1.3); I will write more about it in the next chapter. Just a year later, in 2012, the Groninger Museum devoted a first major exhibition to her work and published the first catalogue with pictures of all her designs from 2008 to 2012.[16] Quite interestingly, the cover very much resembles the cover of the later exhibition *Sculpting the Senses*:

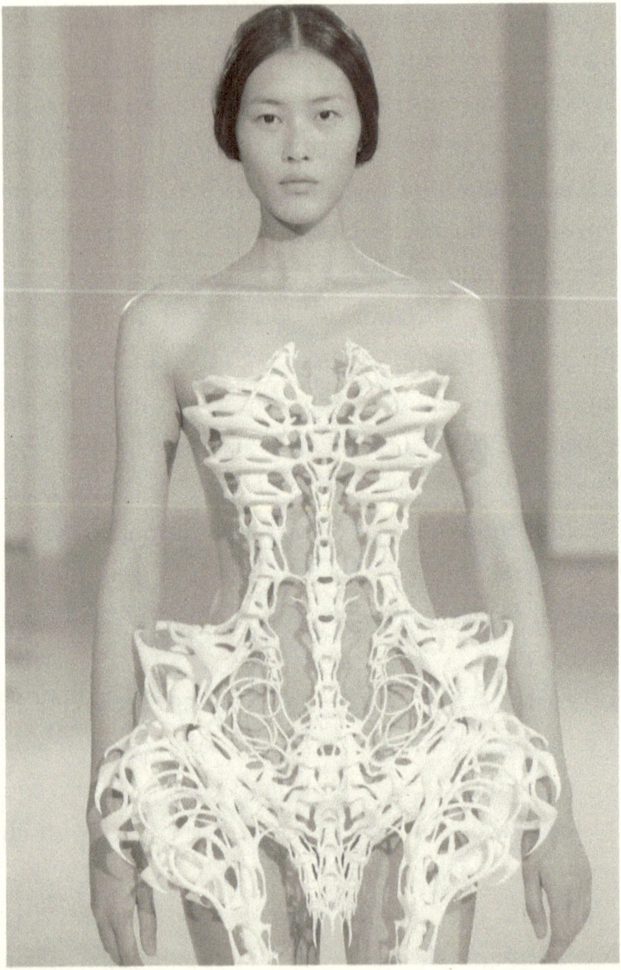

Figure 1.3 Iris van Herpen, collection 'Capriole'; the first fashion show in Paris, A/W 2011. 3D-printed skeleton dress of white polyamide, made in collaboration with architect Isaïe Bloch and 3D printing company Materialise (Sven Hermans). © Photographer Michel Zoeter.

both hard covers are in black and white, featuring a picture of an early white 3D-printed piece embossed on the black cover.

This exhibition later travelled to the United States and was expanded to include the designs till 2015.[17] By now there have been numerous solo exhibitions of her work, while individual designs have been exhibited in fashion or design shows or museums all over the world. The culmination so far has been the highly successful exhibition *Iris van Herpen: Sculpting the Senses*, which was opened by the Dutch Queen Máxima, glamorously dressed in a custom-made 'Gaia' gown by Iris van Herpen, together with France's then first lady, Brigitte Macron, in the Musée des Arts Décoratifs in Paris, 28 November 2023.[18] It was one of the most successful exhibitions in the museum's history, drawing more than 350,000 visitors.[19] The exhibition then travelled to Singapore (2024), Brisbane (2024–25), Rotterdam (2025–26) and in a smaller form to New York (2026). Also at the museum Kunsthal in Rotterdam the exhibition concluded with a record-breaking run, becoming the most visited exhibition in the museum's history with 281,000 visitors.[20]

The Atelier

In a visit to Iris van Herpen's fashion house for haute couture in 2019, I expected sophisticated machines and equipment in the atelier, but there were mainly sewing machines and a few ironing boards.[21] What a surprise: which century was this? The atelier was buzzing with a dozen people who worked with great concentration on the designs for the next fashion show in Paris. The designer Iris van Herpen was working behind computers in a separate room, visible through large windows. The place had the distinct feel of an artist's atelier rather than a slick commercial brand. When I was greeted by the Head of the atelier, Petra Schuddeboom, I saw that she was wearing a self-made pincushion on her wrist – a bricolage of tape and a magnet that holds the pins. Some of the dressmakers in the atelier were sewing 3D-printed pieces together by hand. Pins and needles? I was amazed that Iris van Herpen's technological designs would require them at all. No 3D printers or laser cutters, then, but pins and needles. This was not quite what I expected in the atelier of a designer known for her bold integration of cutting-edge technology into her haute couture. This kind of fashion atelier is rather known from traditional artisans. Still today, her team is small: at its height about 20, mostly young people, work on the creations either for the next exhibition or the next show. With two, three or even four people, they collaborate on the dresses that are draped on the dummies. With needle and thread, they put the finishing touch on Iris van Herpen's creations.

Let me expand on the way that Iris van Herpen creates her designs as I learned during that visit to her atelier. While Iris van Herpen works with advanced technologies, she is both a hands-on and intuitive designer. Iris van Herpen is led by the material(s) through an interaction with the design.[22] She does not make sketches on a piece of paper, because its two-dimensionality does not allow for the complicated details of her designs.[23] In preparing for a new collection, Iris van Herpen and Petra Schuddeboom start working from the material. In the Catalogue for *Sculpting the Senses*, she recounts: 'For each collection, I start by experimenting with new materials.'[24] During the process, they try things out, finding out how the material wants to behave. Their approach is artisanal, using their skills while developing new knowledge and techniques. The global event for fabrics, Première Vision in Paris, is not so important for the Maison because they usually create their own materials, often by combining different techniques and often in collaboration with other artists or technicians from different disciplines. As fashion is created on the human body, they first try a sample out on each other's bodies and on the dummies. By manipulating the material samples, or the samples on the tailor's dummy, they start creating a silhouette or look in the computer. They work with many different computer programmes like Illustrator, Fusion 360, Photoshop, Rhinoceros, Maya, Grasshopper or Marvelous Design. Some of those programmes are actually architectural modelling tools.

It is well known that Iris van Herpen often works with artists, architects and scientists. Yet, in spite of the use of advanced technologies, the design is still subject to an organic interactive process that is different each time. For many, if not most, of her designs, van Herpen insists on the process of moulage: the draping and moulding of the materials and samples on a physical dummy. While it is possible to work on the computer and assess the qualities of the material on a virtual body, make and animate the pattern and get a feel for the expression of the material, the initial steps are most of the time draping the material on the dummy. The feel, look and movement of the material and therefore the moulage process remain important to Iris van Herpen. Only then will the 3D structure be digitally imported and will the silhouette be designed with a computer program. The head of the atelier, Petra Schuddeboom, recounts:

> There are looks that are draped only; looks that are made only in the computer after seeing the sample; looks that are first draped and then manipulated in the computer; and looks for which the process gets repeated a few times for a particular dress. Sometimes a dress is made with one of those processes, but then taken apart and draped again while mixing with other techniques, and then remade. There are so many ways of designing![25]

For Iris van Herpen, technological innovation always goes hand in hand with manual craftsmanship; each design is put together by many hours, weeks or even months of meticulous handwork. Hence the sewing machines in the atelier and the pincushion on the wrist. She even once said: 'For me, handwork is a form of meditation.'[26] To give an example of the hours that go into the handwork: the sculptural red dress that van Herpen designed for Anne Hathaway's character of an ageing pop star in the film *Mother Mary* (2026) took three months of handwork to create.[27] In the movie, however, the costume designer, Sam (Michaela

Coel), crafts the gown overnight, which made Iris van Herpen exclaim 'We need you in the atelier!' when she was joking 'with Ms. Coel about her character's impossible speed'.[28]

While some designs may look computer-designed, they are actually mostly handmade, while other dresses do not have an immediate tech look but are in fact highly technological feats. For example, the flowing silk organza dresses of the later collections are sewn onto bonded frames of Mylar, an innovative material developed by NASA and trademarked by DuPont; to put it simply, it is a form of polyester. Another technique that the Maison uses regularly, and that is also transplanted from architectural manufacturing, is laser cutting. They use this technique often in combination with new materials, such as Mylar, and other forms of polyesters, polyamides and polyurethane. Laser cutting technology helps to generate complex and highly precise patterns. The atelier has also developed a new way of printing rich gradient colours in quite high resolution onto fabric following the layers of the computer drawing. For the colourful dresses of the last few years, ancient techniques of pleating were used together with highly elaborate pattern-making in the computer. By putting together multiple layers of gradient coloured prints, the colourful dresses achieve a 3D effect.

The design process may also be the other way around: an example of quite a spectacular design that looks technological, but is mostly handmade, is the blue dress from 'Shift Souls' (look 13, S/S 2019). The dress is designed in 3D CAD (computer-aided design), but is not 3D printed, although it has the look. The software translates it into 2D, because the companies that cut the many panels need 2D vector files such as .DXF and .AI. The dress consists of 1,100 different panels, which were each numbered, then finished and draped on the dummy. Finally, all the panels were hand-applied to the base; it has a lining that makes it comfortable to wear. The dress involved many hours of handwork for weeks or even a few months by several people, which is not unusual for many of van Herpen's designs. From these descriptions of the design processes, it can be ascertained that Iris van Herpen always designs and makes the dresses in a combination of advanced technologies and artisanal craftsmanship. As she confirms: 'We combine the organic and the synthetic to blur the line between nature, craftsmanship and technology.'[29]

Perhaps it is fitting to end this introduction to the Maison of Iris van Herpen by highlighting what made the *Sculpting the Senses* retrospective so special. One of the most fascinating rooms was the 'Alchemic Atelier', physically at the centre of the exhibition, which recreated a studio as if it were van Herpen's atelier, organised by colour: patches with fine embroidery, organic silicone structures, banana leaves, fossils, pleats, prints and stacked layers of laser-cut organza that together form a three-dimensional wave pattern organised in vibrant colours. The 'Alchemic Atelier' was a veritable *Wunderkammer*, a cabinet of curiosities. Here, the visitor could gasp at a collection of objects not organised by category but by the chromatic code of colour. And visitors did gasp: whenever I visited the exhibition (both in Paris and in Rotterdam), visitors stayed on in this transitional room. Visitors could touch materials, look through microscopes at patches of fabrics or watch instructive videos about how fabrics or designs were made. Let's not forget that these are all invented textiles: created by Iris van Herpen together with artists, scientists and technicians. The visitor was not looking at fabrics like silk or cotton, but at a piece of 'Japanese airfabric that drifts like currents suspended within moon-curved bonings laser-cut from translucent carbon fibre', or a piece of 'upcycled fabric made from marine debris by Parley for the Oceans printed and incised into thousands of fine trilateral tessellations', or 'soft 3D hand-casted PU fabrics that are hand-painted through injection moulding and fine expandable laser-cut Mylar fabrics reminiscent of digital glitches', to quote just a few of the rather overwhelming technological descriptions on Iris van Herpen's website.[30] In this warehouse of futuristic materials, the visitor could admire these assemblages of things: to touch and be touched by the very aliveness of these materials. The 'Alchemic Atelier' functioned very much like the historical '*Wunderkammer*', by raising curiosity while giving information and providing knowledge. The room – which was situated as a passage hall in the middle of the exhibition – also created an archive, keeping memory alive. As Laura Marks writes, 'Memory makes an assemblage with the past; imagination with the future.'[31] The 'Alchemic Atelier' was indeed both a memory bank and a pro-memoria for the future, converging different elements and time zones of past and present.

Sculpting the Senses was constructed as an immersive experience around nine themes that recur throughout her oeuvre, such as 'Synaesthesia', 'Growth Systems' or 'Mythology of Fear'. The rooms were set up thematically instead of chronologically: a dress from 2007 was put next to a dress from 2023, which emphasises how consistent her aesthetic style has been over the last two decades. The haute couture pieces were accompanied by contemporary art, videos and items from the natural sciences. Fossils, skeletons and shells from the natural world were juxtaposed to works by artists like Casey Curran, Ferruccio Laviani and Janaina Mello Landini, who have either inspired or collaborated with Iris van Herpen over the years. The artist Rogan Brown, for example, made five fragile structures of paper for the exhibition, reminiscent of the fine laser cuttings of van Herpen's dresses. The Japanese art collective Mé shaped shiny black waves as a fitting foundation for the theme 'Water and Dreams'.

Musician, artist and van Herpen's partner Salvador Breed created a specific sound composition for the exhibition (he is also responsible for the music of her catwalk shows). The ambient sound design worked very well in making the different themes come to life: a tapping sound in the skeleton hall or a swingy hum around the designs that were inspired by electricity.

Soundscapes are essential in the sense that they are transversal, trans-historical and trans-media, and they always include a non-human element, be it the trains, the wind of computer-generated sounds or just the sound of instruments. The combination of fashion designs, artworks, exhibits from nature and science, together with the ambient soundscape, not only enhanced the aesthetics of van Herpen's designs but also gave a glimpse into her interdisciplinary creativity. The particular design of this exhibition thus gave an insight into the unique way in which van Herpen mixes sartorial craftsmanship with cutting-edge technologies, inspired by the beauty of art, nature and science.

The last room, featuring the theme of 'Cosmic Bloom', exhibited van Herpen's most colourful dresses in an installation that truly defied gravity – mimicking the experience of parachute jumping and skydiving that fascinates Iris van Herpen so much.[32] The dresses floated upside down and sideways through the room. This spectacular ending of the exhibition fits in with the more recent designs of the last few years that evoke a constant sense of fluidity and dynamic energy. Her fashion design 'is timeless and placeless precisely because of her unique fusion of hand and technology and her crossing over of borders of knowledge, knowing and sensing'.[33] In the following chapters I will show how Iris van Herpen's innovative designs foreground the vibrancy of matter and the dynamics of time in a style that I call 'posthuman'.

Notes

1 The information in this chapter is put together from different sources: the website of Maison Iris van Herpen (https://www.irisvanherpen.com/about/the-maison); the Catalogue *Iris van Herpen: Sculpting the Senses*. (Amsterdam: Lannoo, 2023); and the Dutch podcast series by Splinter Chabot for Museum Kunsthal Rotterdam, 2025. In 2019, I visited Iris van Herpen's atelier in Amsterdam and interviewed the head of the atelier, Petra Schuddeboom; and (then) commercial director Paul van As, who both gave me valuable information about the way in which the small team in the studio works and about the process of designing. Unfortunately, the Atelier did not have the time to accommodate a second visit in 2026 as their team is very small; the team answered some (but not all) of my questions by email.

2 Hans Ulrich Obrist, 'Interview with Iris van Herpen' in Catalogue *Iris van Herpen: Sculpting the Senses.* (Amsterdam: Lannoo, 2023), 29.

3 These collections are best represented in Iris van Herpen, Catalogue *Exhibition Iris van Herpen.* (Groningen: Groninger Museum and BAI Publishers, 2012).

4 Ibid., n.p.

5 Obrist, Catalogue *Iris van Herpen: Sculpting the Senses*, 29.

6 Quoted in Andrew Bolton, *Manus x Machina: Fashion in an Age of Technology.* (New York: The Metropolitan Museum of Art, 2016), xviii.

7 Interview with the head of the atelier, Petra Schuddeboom, 3 September 2019.

8 Ibid.

9 Vanessa Gerrie, *Borderless Fashion Practice: Contemporary Fashion in the Metamodern Age.* (New Brunswick: Rutgers University Press, 2023), 121.

10 Cloé Pitiot, in Catalogue *Iris van Herpen: Sculpting the Senses.* (Amsterdam: Lannoo, 2023), 15.

11 Anneke Smelik, 'Cybercouture: The Fashionable Technology of Pauline van Dongen, Iris van Herpen and Bart Hess' in *Delft Blue to Denim Blue. Contemporary Dutch Fashion*, ed. Anneke Smelik. (London: I.B. Tauris/Bloomsbury, 2017), 252–269.

12 Ninke Bloemberg (ed.), *Het Nieuwe Ambacht: Iris van Herpen en haar inspiratie* ['The New Craft: Iris van Herpen and Her Inspiration']. (Utrecht: Centraal Museum, 2011), 11, my translation.
13 Interview with (then) commercial director Paul van As, 19 January 2019.
14 Louise Curtis in Catalogue *Iris van Herpen: Sculpting the Senses.* (Amsterdam: Lannoo, 2023), 47.
15 https://www.irisvanherpen.com/news.
16 Herpen, Catalogue *Exhibition Iris van Herpen.*
17 Catalogue *Iris van Herpen: Transforming Fashion.* The catalogue was co-published by the High Museum of Art, Atlanta, and the Groninger Museum, 2015.
18 Anneke Smelik, 'Exhibition Review of *Iris van Herpen: Sculpting the Senses*'. *Critical Studies in Fashion & Beauty* 15, no. 2 (2024): 245–249. https://doi.org/10.1386/csfb_00080_5.
19 Deirdre McQuillan, 'Visionary Designer Iris Van Herpen Combines Technology with Craftsmanship in Ways Like No Other'. *The Irish Times,* 19 August 2024. https://www.irishtimes.com/life-style/fashion/2024/08/19/visionary-designer-iris-van-herpen-combines-technology-with-craftsmanship-in-ways-like-no-other/.
20 Ibid.
21 Anneke Smelik, 'Fractal Folds: The Posthuman Fashion of Iris van Herpen'. *Fashion Theory* 26, no. 1 (2022): 5–26. https://doi.org/10.1080/1362704X.2020.1850035.
22 Ibid.
23 Bloemberg, *Het Nieuwe Ambacht*, 10, my translation.
24 Obrist, Catalogue *Iris van Herpen: Sculpting the Senses*, 28.
25 Interview with Petra Schuddeboom, 2019; see for further elaboration, Smelik, 'Fractal Folds'.
26 Quoted in Bolton, *Manus x Machina*, xvii.
27 Kellina Moore, 'Designing for a Pop Star'. *The New York Times*, 17 April 2026. https://www.nytimes.com/2026/04/17/style/mother-mary-costumes-iris-van-herpen.html?smid=url-share.
28 Ibid.
29 Quoted in Obrist, Catalogue *Iris van Herpen: Sculpting the Senses*, 29.

30 https://www.irisvanherpen.com/. Quotes taken from the editorials of respectively the collections 'Sympoeisis' (A/W 2025), 'Roots of Rebirth' (S/S 2021), and 'Between the Lines' (S/S 2017).

31 Laura U. Marks, *The Fold: From Your Body to the Cosmos.* (Durham: Duke University Press, 2024), 43.

32 Obrist, Catalogue *Iris van Herpen: Sculpting the Senses*, 29.

33 Ariane Koek, 'On the Edge of the Im/Material' in Catalogue *Iris van Herpen: Sculpting the Senses.* (Amsterdam: Lannoo, 2023), 235.

Chapter 2

A 3D-PRINTED DRESS

In this chapter, I look at van Herpen's groundbreaking adoption of 3D printing, a development that established her international reputation as one of fashion's foremost innovators. I discuss the technologies underlying 3D printing and consider how they inform some of her most experimental creations. To contextualise these developments, I draw on the theoretical perspectives of new materialism and posthumanism, both of which frame her practice as an ongoing negotiation between human and non-human forces. Viewed through this lens, van Herpen's work articulates a posthuman aesthetic that dissolves boundaries between nature and culture, as well as between the biological and the technological.

Iris van Herpen is the first fashion designer to use three-dimensional printing technology in her designs. Van Herpen's white 3D-printed top for her 2010 collection 'Crystallisation' was first shown to the public at the Arnhem Fashion Biennale in 2011. This very first 3D-printed piece, with its otherworldly design, made van Herpen famous and featured as the cover image for the catalogue of the exhibition *Sculpting the Senses* (see Figure 1.2).[1] A year later, the design was launched again as look 16 in van Herpen's first haute couture collection presented in Paris, 'Capriole' (A/W 2011).[2]

The sheer brilliance of this strange form calls forth a sense of awe and inspiration: Is it mimicking or remaking coral, shell, crystal? Is it a snail or a fossil, or both? Could it actually be worn on a human body? The organic forms are clearly inspired by biology and palaeontology, and can be seen as natural matter, or variations on organic 'nature'. Yet, the inorganic technology of 3D printing was at the time overwhelming, because it was entirely new. This revolutionary innovation is one of the reasons why she is so often called a visionary.[3]

Van Herpen made the organic, fossil- or shell-like structure of the 3D-printed top in collaboration with architect Daniel Widrig. Rapid prototyping enabled them to materialise digital designs with a 3D printer, producing elaborate folds without the need for needle and thread. That alone transcends the natural domain and takes the designer beyond what is commonly feasible in dressmaking. The new technologies of digital designing and 3D printing allow the designer to create forms that are impossible to design by a 2D drawing, resulting in an intricacy of three-dimensional folds that is truly unique. And there lies the fatal attraction of van Herpen's quest for a space in-between nature and culture, matter and technology. In an interview with Andrew Bolton, she explains: 'With 3D printing, I am very much drawn to the organic, [...] because in organic structures such as fossils, for instance, you have structures that you can't easily replicate by hand.'[4] But that love for the organic is mediated and can only be asserted through technological mediation. As early then as in 2010, van Herpen was developing her experimental innovative style, always moving back and forth between sartorial craftsmanship and cutting-edge technology, designing in-between the organic and inorganic.[5] Elsewhere, she has referred to her sculptural designs as 'organic futurism'.[6] This is a very effective term, as it precisely hints at that special combination of finding inspiration in nature while experimenting with new, futuristic technologies.

A year later, the Centraal Museum Utrecht (Netherlands) commissioned a 3D-printed dress from Iris van Herpen in 2011 that she developed again with architect Daniel Widrig and was produced by 3D print company Materialise. It is part of the 'Escapism' collection (S/S 2011), and its intricate shell-like or lace-like structure was a predecessor of the skeleton design that she made with architect Isaïe Bloch in the same year.[7] The aesthetics of the first two 3D-printed pieces, the top and the Escapism dress (designed with Widrig), feature repetitions in their forms. The skeleton dress (designed with Isaïe Bloch; see Figure 1.3) has more organic and complex forms that mimic the flow of a living body.[8] The newness of all of these early 3D-printed designs stood out at the time. Moreover, the exuberant and intricate folds create a sense of wonder. Folds and foldings are a typical stylistic feature of van Herpen's aesthetics that I will discuss further in the next chapter.

The aesthetics or rather the architectural structure of the 'Escapism' dress (Figure 2.1) is equally reminiscent of a skeleton – a style that became highly prominent in Iris van Herpen's designs throughout her career: outside-in becomes inside-out, almost like a skeleton worn in front of the human body, making the invisible visible. The dress comes apart in several pieces and is designed for the front and back of the upper body. It looks like a piece of sculpture, but its sculptural form is made for a human body that moves. Here again, the 'organic futurism' of the design is inspired by nature, but made with cutting-edge technologies. The dress became an instant success and was named as one of the 50 best inventions of 2011 by *Time Magazine*, which called it a 'fantastical' dress.[9] This dress, the 3D-printed top, and the skeleton dress were all part of Iris van Herpen's debut show 'Capriole' in Paris in 2011.

The 3D-printed 'Escapism' dress was commissioned for an exhibition entitled 'The New Craft' that took place in 2011 in the Centraal Museum Utrecht in the Netherlands. This was the very first exhibition, curated by Ninke Bloemberg, to focus on the experimental work of Iris van Herpen and her sources of inspiration. Works by artists who inspired van Herpen at the time, such as Kris Kuksi, Nanine Linning, Stephen Jones, Bart Hess and Irene Bussemaker, were exhibited alongside works from the Centraal Museum's applied arts collection. As Iris van Herpen says: 'It's a dream of mine to work with artists

Figure 2.1 Iris van Herpen, collection 'Escapism', S/S 2011. White 3D-printed dress with lace-like structure made in collaboration with architect Daniel Widrig. 3D printing: .MGX by Materialise. © Photographer Michel Zoeter. The dress was named one of the best inventions by *Time Magazine* in 2011.

who inspire me. To work with others and bring fashion back to a valuable product by exploring new forms, materials, and techniques within the field of fashion.'[10] During a field trip to the archive of the Centraal Museum Utrecht that I made in 2018, I could view and touch this dress and other designs.[11] As with the other 3D-printed tops and dresses of that year, the material is polyamide. The material was indeed very hard and cold to the touch and must be quite uncomfortable to wear. Yet, its novelty was – and still is – exciting.

The production process of 3D printing is documented in a short Dutch film by Wendy van Wilgenburg, specially curated by the Centraal Museum.[12] The dress was initially planned in the computer, then still in Photoshop. Later, Iris van Herpen also uses other computer programmes, like Illustrator, Fusion 360, Rhinoceros, Grasshopper, Maya or Marvelous Designer. We should not forget that 3D printing is a technique originally more apt for architecture than for fashion (it was initially also used in the medical field as a way of rapidly creating prototypes). Many of these computer programmes are in fact tools for creating architectural prototyping systems. It is therefore no surprise that for the early 3D-printed tops and dresses, she worked with an architect to develop a 3D model. For the 'Escapism' dress, Daniel Widrich and Iris van Herpen used the 3D printing technique of Selective Laser Sintering. This is a technique by which parts are built layer by layer with a fine polymer powder. Successive powder layers are spread on top of each other and, after each layer, a laser beam scans the surface and binds together ('sinters') the powder involved in the design. The remaining powder is easily dusted or air-brushed away when the design is removed from the machine.[13] Iris van Herpen writes that 'each layer is horizontally printed to a 0.1 mm thickness and therefore took six days of continuous printing'.[14] While the process results in a ready-to-wear dress that is an exact replica of the original sketched version, it is, all in all, labour-intensive work. The difference with handwork is that one can always change the design and keep working on it, whereas when a 3D-printed piece comes out of the machine, its design cannot be changed anymore.

Iris van Herpen was quite aware of the limitations of 3D printing: '[...] the limitation for me at the moment is the materials – their quality and flexibility [...] I started out printing in polyamide, which is flexible when you print it thin and long, however when you begin to print a surface it is quite rigid'.[15] She still hoped for 3D materials to become more flexible, which did indeed happen around that time. However, she found a way of making the rigid material more flexible: 'A difficulty for me is that I can fall in love with a material but then I can't use it because it is rigid.'[16] She learned another way of working with rigid material: '[...] if I break it down into smaller pieces and combine it with something more flexible'.[17] This happened in the 3D-printed collections like 'Voltage' (S/S 2013) and 'Wilderness Embodied' (A/W 2013), when van Herpen had further mastered the technique of 3D printing and materials had become more flexible.

New Materialism

Fashion scholar and curator Valerie Steele admonishes that 'tape measures, scales, and magnifying glasses are useful tools' to 'read' a garment.[18] However, when I studied Iris van Herpen's 3D-printed 'Escapism' dress in the archive of the Centraal Museum Utrecht in 2018, it is striking to note that the fashion curator, Ninke Bloemberg, and I were rather confused as to what was back to front or up and down. We could not make much sense of the different 3D-printed pieces that we were holding in our hands without looking at an image of a model wearing them. Touching the hard material also did not give much information about the kind of 'fabric' or technology we were confronted with, although we could see the white polyamide had been smeared with the make-up of the model who wore it on the catwalk. Although we measured the garment (length 120 cm, width 60 cm, depth 60 cm), the conventional tools of object-based dress studies seemed to fall short to even begin to describe this garment of intricate folds. In fact, at the time, I took all the technical information from the documentary mentioned above.

My investigative experience in the museum's archive shows that technological innovations like the one that Iris van Herpen continues to develop and explore require new methods of analysis and new theoretical concepts. This extra critical effort is due to the transformative and 'weird' structure of van Herpen's work, which defies established parameters in cultural enquiry and fashion analyses. Innovation is therefore also required of the critics and readers of her provocative creations. Meeting this intellectual challenge, and inspired by Iris van Herpen's otherworldly designs, I have introduced 'new materialism' as a new method,[19] and 'the posthuman' as a new theoretical concept.[20] I will briefly explain both frameworks here as groundwork for my interpretation of Iris van Herpen's designs.

On a first, rather practical level, a new materialist method of analysis gives priority to an enhanced appreciation of the material and sensory aspects of fashion. Fashion, perhaps more conspicuously than other cultural realms, consists of material objects and involves a bodily practice of dressing. That seems obvious, till you try to apply that insight to the job of critically reviewing the fashion objects in question: All sorts of implications and applications jump out at you and force a reconsideration of the basic terms of criticism and analysis. Paying attention to the material aspects of a fashion design, as I did above, is therefore not enough. Materiality needs to be pushed to the understanding of the objects involved in this process. Van Herpen's work challenges those assumptions, also in the ways they affect the viewers and the critics. This kind of couture forces us to think further and harder about who the subject and what the object is.

This is where new materialism introduces the notion of material agency.[21] This idea does not refer to agency in the strictly humanist sense of 'will' or 'intention', which implicitly assumes an anthropomorphic subject and an anthropocentric world view. It is rather the case that matter itself should be seen as an active agent, capable of 'doing' things, in the sense of acting upon other entities in the world. After all, contemporary science – physics and genetics – teaches us that we are all made of the same matter, through different compositions. Such an insight entails recognising some form of agency in non-human actors, of the organic and the inorganic kind – from cotton to man-made fibres, knitted wool to smart fabrics, solar dresses to 3D-printed garments – bringing the dynamics of fashion to the fore. They all have their own degree and speed and force upon the world. Matter has an active presence, which we humans tend to reduce to an instrumental function, whereas it is much more than that. Laura Marks heeds that we need 'to overcome the prejudice against humanmade things as lacking life'.[22] And if this sounds abstract, we all know that materials 'do things' to us, in the sense of impacting on our embodied existence. For example, jeans may be too tight and hence uncomfortable, silk may soothe our skin, a woollen sweater may itch, while a polyamide top of Iris van Herpen may feel very hard and inflexible on the wearer's body. This idea of material agency is manifestly relational, in the sense that it also involves attention to the interaction with the very materiality of the human body as vibrant and intelligent matter; I will come back to this issue in the chapter on Iris van Herpen's designs for dancers.

A second level of a new materialist approach starts from the continuum between nature and culture that I already mentioned in the Introduction, and it concerns the acknowledgement of the pivotal role of technology in fashion design today. Van

Herpen's designs show how material agency – the shaping of living matter and materials – can be performed by and with technology in such a way that it can no longer be understood as a strictly human prerogative. The extravagant forms and shapes of van Herpen's artistic vision draw attention to the technological details of the designs, showing that materiality is active and productive. The combination of traditional manual craftsmanship and innovative technologies not only allows van Herpen to focus greater attention on the material aspects of high-performance fibres, smart fabrics or innovative techniques but also opens up engaged and meaning-making interconnections with the human body. New materialism would then define her designs as hybrid assemblages of fibres, materials, skin and body, organic and inorganic tied together in a techno-environmental embrace of vast speed and scale.

A third level of new materialist insight brings us to yet a deeper level. In the view of new materialists, 'matter' is an emergent and dynamic flow that forever changes and transforms. This – perhaps radical – idea has been argued by scholars like Tim Ingold and Jane Bennett.[23] They write eloquently of the vitality of things, of the 'vibrant materiality' of things,[24] or as Laura Marks writes: 'Matter is responsive and active.'[25] Just like nature forever changes and transforms, so do materials and technologies. New materialism then works from a dynamic notion of life in which human bodies, fibres, fabrics, garments and technologies are inextricably entangled. Such a novel perspective permits a broader understanding of Iris van Herpen's designs as materially co-produced in a complex network of interconnected human and non-human actors. It also provides new terminology and forms of representation for this experimental approach. And she says so much herself: 'I believe science, fashion and biology should grow together', as they can 'spiritually shape our human experience'.[26]

Posthuman Aesthetics

This brings me to the concept of the posthuman, which is closely related to the philosophical school of new materialism.[27] The posthuman is basically a hybrid figure; it is about thinking what the human is or, rather, becomes, in a world that is both biological, environmentally grounded and highly technological. Posthuman philosophy proposes a non-anthropocentric view by taking the human subject away from the centre of attention in thought and cultural critique.[28] It challenges any suggestion of a hierarchical relation between the human and the non-human entities, both organic and technological. Rather, a posthuman perspective acknowledges a nature–culture continuum, such as between the human and its many others – the non-human. It also stresses the affirmative potential of such a collaborative bond.

The non-human can be organic or inorganic; nature or technology. Traditionally, the non-human refers to the organic world: to trees, animals or monsters, as well as to bacteria, fungi or spiders. Today, the non-human equally pertains to the technological or inorganic world of machines, robotics, 3D printing and artificial intelligence. In the case of fashion, as we saw above, the non-human can be made of organic materials like wool, silk and cotton, or of technological materials like polymer fibres, solar cells or 3D-printed polyamide. In her practice, we usually find a mix of natural fibres like wool, silk and cotton and synthetic ones like Mylar, polyurethane and silicone. This sustained focus on the non-human is crucial for van Herpen's designs; in fact, her work is almost a commentary on the new posthuman environment that we have created. For example, she refers to her collection 'Shift Souls' (S/S 2019) as reflecting

> a posthuman world in which the boundaries between human and non-human, natural and artificial, dissolve. The emerging technologies of synthetic biology and genetic engineering have the potential to create new forms of life that are not bound by traditional categories of biology or identity, both positively and negatively. Similarly, my use of innovative materials and technologies challenges assumptions about what is natural and what is artificial.[29]

The posthuman methodological move of decentring the human is of course highly relevant in the context of the climate crisis and environmental degradation, which incidentally are made worse by the fast fashion industry. But here I want to concentrate on posthuman aesthetics. By being designed for the human body, fashion conventionally focuses on the human figure in a serviceable, user-friendly way. Yet, a posthuman aesthetic makes that body strange and otherworldly as it deliberately pursues unfamiliar and estranging effects. In this context, it is no surprise that in 2022 Iris van Herpen was invited to design a few costumes for the science fiction film *Black Panther: Wakanda Forever* (directed by Ryan Coogler). She made a custom ceremonial look for Letitia Wright (who plays Shuri) and a ceremonial cape for Mabel Cadena (playing Namora), under the supervision of the costume designer Ruth E. Carter.[30]

Coming back to van Herpen's first 3D-printed designs, like the skeleton dress, we can see how the designs point to alien shapes and the fantastical. The theme of the exoskeleton runs through van Herpen's designs from the beginning of her career till today. It is quite a haunting design – as if the body has been turned inside out by wearing the bones in front of the body. Bridging the digital (design in the computer), the technological (3D printing, polyamide material) and the physical (the female body), van Herpen's designs present bodies as posthuman figures in a nature–culture continuum. She shows how the human is deeply entangled with the wider material world, both organically and technologically. By making alliances with the non-human, she denaturalises the human body, yet presents the technology as a new protective frame. Inventing a posthuman aesthetic means to 'do' something to the human body, to enhance it, transform it and blend it with the new environments we are inhabiting in today's world. Iris van Herpen confirms: 'I love working with 3D printing because it is so unlimited in the complexity and colours.'[31]

Take, for instance, Iris van Herpen's *Biophilia* dress from the collection 'Escapism' (S/S 2011; see Figure 2.2), designed together with architect Daniel Widrig and inspired by the baroque sculptural work of American artist Kris Kuksi.[32] In its blue variant, the dress was custom-made for Icelandic singer Björk for her *Biophilia* tour in 2012; van Herpen continued to design for Björk's performances in later years.[33] I write 'blue dress', but is this a dress? Its bizarre forms are shaped by laser-cut semi-transparent acrylic sheets forming spherical shapes that bulge in strange places on the body. The grotesque shell-like shapes deform the human figure in a thought-provoking manner. The unfamiliar forms indicate an escape from the normativity of the (mostly female) body, from conventional naturalistic representations, sanctioned by centuries of art historical canonical conventions and the dominance of the Western beauty ideal in fashion. As the title of the collection, 'Escapism', suggests, these designs escape from everyday reality. For this design, van Herpen was inspired by the fantastical paintings of the late-medieval Dutch painter Hieronymus Bosch (1450–1516).[34]

Designs like the Biophilia dress, the snake dress or the bird dress point to the grotesque and the fantastic. In the *Sculpting the Senses* retrospective, these and other fantastical dresses were gathered under the theme of 'Mythology of Fear', inspired by paintings by Bosch or by Greek myths. They divulge her

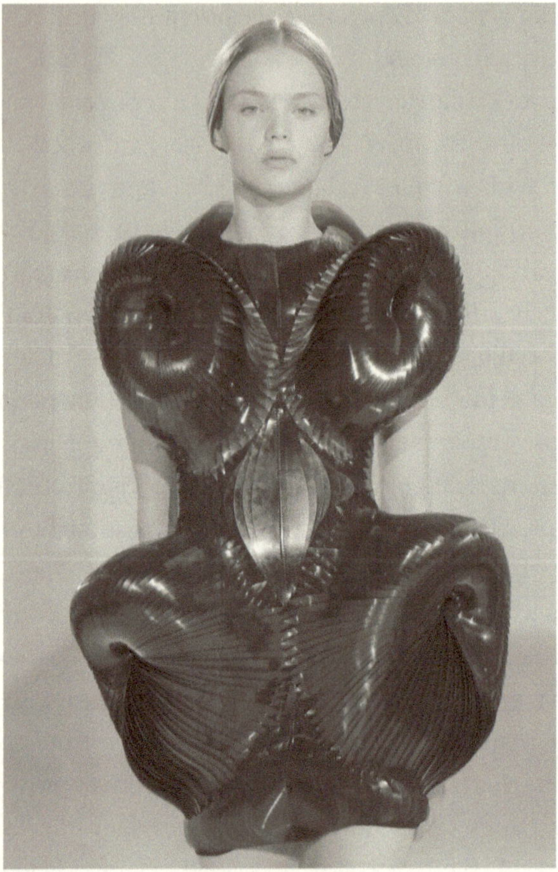

Figure 2.2 Iris van Herpen, collection 'Escapism', S/S 2011. Black dress made of acrylic, nylon, metal, formed from semi-transparent acrylic sheets that have been hand- and laser-cut and mounted onto a tulle ground to create a shell-like shape. The dress fastens down centre back with a long metal zip. Collaboration with architect Isaïe Bloch. 3D printing partner: Materialise (Sven Hermans). © Photographer Michel Zoeter.

penchant for mystery and eccentricity.[35] As in many of her other designs, van Herpen manages to denaturalise the human body and make it weird: inside-out, with lumps and bumps in odd places, shrouded in smoke, covered in 3D-printed spikes, snowflakes or eerie feathers, or cloaked in circular shapes and geometric patterns made of silicone, polyamide, metal or glass. This is the most radical impact of her posthuman aesthetic: the alienating and haunting denaturalisation of the human figure through technological mediation and new materials.[36] And yet, at the same time, the designs are attractive, mesmerising even; it makes you want to go there and make friends with this brave new world.

The process of combining the organic and the inorganic creates a dissonant effect that produces energy. The strident lack of harmony is not solved in an established form of closure by pleasing aesthetics, but by jarring forms refiguring the body. By deconstructive ways of dressing, high-end fashion designers like van Herpen and daring performers like Björk can move beyond merely representing the familiar contours of the human body and therefore beyond fixed forms of identity. Van Herpen's designs gain therefore by being understood as examples of posthuman bodies. Through the high-tech designs, the models transcend the boundaries of what a body can look like, becoming in-between characters.

Looking at any of van Herpen's innovative and 'monstrous' designs, one can see how the posthuman body is dynamic, opening up to a multiplicity of intertwined lines, notches, gaps and fissures that together form a vortex, a maze or web. Featuring a posthuman style of dynamic in-betweenness – the human and the non-human – Iris van Herpen helps to dress a posthuman body that is organically traversed by technology and new materials. The contrast of producing organic structures with the latest technologies creates a posthuman aesthetic – an aesthetic that is post-naturalistic, enacting a nature–culture continuum. To finish this chapter in her own words:

> This embodies my vision of the interconnectedness of all things, understanding the complexity of connection and transformation through time with all the elements around us, which move across different scales and dimensions. In much of my work I try to reveal the invisible connections that exist between all the different layers of life. And I believe that through art we can show these layers, so we can engage with the natural world on a deeper level. Some designs are made to only reflect light in movement, to sense a seemingly absence of matter, like looking at a cloud dancing in front of the skin.[37]

Notes

1 Iris van Herpen, Catalogue *Iris van Herpen: Sculpting the Senses.* (Amsterdam: Lannoo, 2023).

2 Unfortunately, van Herpen's website no longer features all collections in its archive and has merged the earlier collections of 2010 and

2011. Not only are many of the early collections no longer stored online but individual pieces have changed numbers and collections: While this white 3D-printed top was the last (unnumbered) look in 2010, it was look 11 in 2011. On the website, it is now look 16 in the collection 'Capriole', which brings together designs from several years. See 'Capriole', Iris van Herpen, https://www.irisvanherpen.com/collections/capriole/runway-17.

3 For example, Bradley Quinn, *Fashion Futures*. (London: Merrell, 2012), 12; Christine Macel, 'Foreword' in Catalogue *Iris van Herpen: Sculpting the Senses*. (Amsterdam: Lannoo, 2023), 11; Deirdre McQuillan, 'Visionary Designer Iris Van Herpen Combines Technology with Craftsmanship in Ways Like No Other'. *The Irish Times*, 19 August 2024. https://www.irishtimes.com/life-style/fashion/2024/08/19/visionary-designer-iris-van-herpen-combines-technology-with-craftsmanship-in-ways-like-no-other/.

4 Quoted in Andrew Bolton, *Manus x Machina: Fashion in an Age of Technology*. (New York: The Metropolitan Museum of Art, 2016), xvii.

5 Anneke Smelik, 'A Dance of Materials: Between the Organic and Inorganic in Iris van Herpen's Fashion'. *National Gallery of Victoria Art Journal*, Australia, 11 December 2023.

6 Quoted in Ninke Bloemberg (ed.), *Het Nieuwe Ambacht: Iris van Herpen en haar inspiratie* ['The New Craft: Iris van Herpen and Her Inspiration']. (Utrecht: Centraal Museum, 2011), 13, my translation.

7 The dress is no longer shown on Iris van Herpen's website. It can be found online in the collection of the Centraal Museum: https://collectie.centraalmuseum.nl/details/collection/35476.

8 Source: Iris van Herpen in the documentary film of Centraal Museum: https://youtu.be/eNlgpaA9KO4?si=3jWd--W2iUG8uSm7.

9 *Time Magazine*. 'The Invention Issue', 28 November 2011, n.p. https://time.com/archive/6640671/the-50-best-inventions/.

10 Quoted in Bloemberg, *Het Nieuwe Ambacht*, 12, my translation.

11 See for further elaboration, Anneke Smelik, 'New Materialism: A Theoretical Framework for Fashion in the Age of Technological Innovation'. *International Journal of Fashion Studies* 5, no. 1 (2018): 33–54. https://doi.org/10.1386/infs.5.1.33_1.

12 This particular video is about 3D printing the skeleton dress. Available on YouTube: https://youtu.be/eNlgpaA9KO4?si=3jWd--W2iUG8uSm7.

13 See for a description of the process: https://www.materialise.com/en/inspiration/cases/iris-van-herpen.

14 van Herpen, Catalogue *Iris van Herpen: Sculpting the Senses*, 127.

15 Iris van Herpen, *A Magazine Curated by Iris van Herpen*. No. A13. (Antwerp: A Publisher, 2014), 26.

16 Ibid.

17 Ibid.

18 Valerie Steele, 'A Museum of Fashion Is More Than a Clothes-Bag'. *Fashion Theory* 2, no. 4 (1998): 329.

19 Smelik, 'New Materialism', 33–54; Agnès Rocamora and Anneke Smelik, 'Introduction' in *Thinking Through Fashion: A Guide to Key Theorists*, 2nd ed., ed. Agnès Rocamora and Anneke Smelik. (London: Bloomsbury, 2025), 1–26.

20 Anneke Smelik, 'A Posthuman Turn in Fashion' in *Routledge Companion to Fashion Studies*, ed. V. Manlow, E. Paulicelli and E. Wissinger. (New York: Routledge, 2021), 57–64; and Anneke Smelik, 'Fractal Folds: The Posthuman Fashion of Iris van Herpen'. *Fashion Theory* 26, no. 1 (2022): 5–26.

21 Smelik, 'New Materialism', 33–54.

22 Laura U. Marks, *The Fold: From Your Body to the Cosmos*. (Durham: Duke University Press, 2024), 42.

23 Tim Ingold, 'Toward an Ecology of Materials'. *Annual Review of Anthropology* 41 (2012): 427–442; Jane Bennett, *Vibrant Matter: A Political Ecology of Things*. (Durham: Duke University Press, 2010).

24 Bennett *Vibrant Matter*, viii.

25 Marks, *The Fold*, 40.

26 Quoted in Hans Ulrich Obrist, 'Interview with Iris van Herpen' in Catalogue *Iris van Herpen: Sculpting the Senses*. (Amsterdam: Lannoo, 2023), 29.

27 Smelik, 'A Posthuman Turn in Fashion'.

28 Rosi Braidotti, *The Posthuman*. (Cambridge: Polity Press, 2013).

29 Iris van Herpen quoted in Obrist, Catalogue *Iris van Herpen: Sculpting the Senses*, 33.
30 https://www.irisvanherpen.com/news/-47.
31 *A Magazine Curated by Iris van Herpen*. No. A13, 26.
32 Catalogue *Exhibition Iris van Herpen*. (Groningen: Groninger Museum and BAI Publishers, 2012), n.p. Van Herpen's website no longer shows the 'Escapism' collection of 2011. This dress is now featured as part of the 'Capriole' collection; a version in black is shown as look 18. See: https://www.irisvanherpen.com/collections/capriole/runway-17.
33 The National Gallery of Victoria (Australia) has a blue version of the dress in its collection. See the description: https://www.ngv.vic.gov.au/explore/collection/work/121972/.
34 Catalogue *Iris van Herpen: Sculpting the Senses*, 160.
35 Ibid.
36 Smelik, 'Fractal Folds'.
37 Quoted in Obrist, Catalogue *Iris van Herpen: Sculpting the Senses*, 32.

Chapter 3

FOLDS

In this chapter, I turn to one of the most consistent stylistic elements in van Herpen's work: the fold. Folds – like pleats, bends, loops, waves, circles, wrinkles, bows, knots, draperies, rhizomes – tend to recur in her designs with great regularity. Drawing on Gilles Deleuze's notion of the fold, I investigate its varied meanings and conceptual implications. The fold operates as a profoundly expressive form; its movements evoke emotion, expansion and openness, positioning the subject within an ongoing process of becoming rather than a fixed state. Through this motif, van Herpen presents transformation as continuous, with both garment and wearer folding, unfolding, enfolding and refolding in a perpetual state of metamorphosis.

Take, for instance, the vibrant red gown that Iris van Herpen designed for Anne Hathaway's character in the film *Mother Mary* (2026). Moore describes how the garment's structure is defined by tiny micro-pleats, achieved by folding the fabric into paper moulds shaped precisely as desired, before baking them in the oven to fix the form.[1] The result is a dress featuring prominent folds that contour the chest, billowing dramatically at the hips and back and finally transitioning into a softer skirt that gradually dissolves into black. Iris van Herpen claims: 'This dress is actually not really a dress – it's a spirit. It's something from another dimension.'[2]

A fold may perhaps not be spiritual, but it is always exuberant. A fold wraps around itself, creating a semi-enclosed space that vibrates – folding, unfolding, enfolding, refolding. Opening in, opening out. The folds instigate a never-ending process of movement: folding in, doubling over, folding open, pulling out, folding up. Folds hide within folds. Folding implies en- and unfolding, showing that inside-out and outside-in are just the boundary edge of a continuous surface that supports complex forms and multiple spaces.

Van Herpen's designs present a veritable cascade of intricate folds and detailed enfoldings. Not unlike the sculptures of the Baroque – made world-famous by the Italian sculptor Gianlorenzo Bernini – van Herpen's style mimics organic forms like a waft of smoke, a splash of water, a ring of twisted leaves, spider webs, honeycombs, shells, coral reefs or rhizomic roots, imprints of a human hand on living flesh. Her designs present a unique play of neo-baroque shapes that wrap, buckle, bend and coil, undulating and fluctuating. Materials ripple, waver and swing as if they were still free from the restraints of designed form, or perhaps, yearned to return to the pure flows of matter.

Movement is ever so important to van Herpen's designs, but it is never one-directional.

This distinctive sensibility is both captured and enhanced by the choice of traditional flowing fabrics like silk, satin, tulle or organza. It is also reiterated by the preference for materials such as silicone, leather, metal, plastic, glass, synthetic polyesters and hi-tech fabrics, which enable contemporary digital and advanced technologies to produce extraordinarily complex and intricate shapes, forms and surfaces.[3]

The combination of a digitalised designing process and three-dimensional printing allows for these inimitable folds: Many of the intricate forms are impossible to sketch on a two-dimensional piece of paper.[4] The earliest 3D-printed designs of the complicated folds were made of hard and stiff materials like polyamide, as in 'Capriole' (A/W 2011) and 'Escapism' (S/S 2011), discussed in the previous chapter. As soon as the technology of 3D printing further advanced, the garments gradually became more flexible. The soft folds are enabled by the plasticity of new materials created by super-polymers or nanomaterials that make new forms possible in glass or ceramics, metallic fibres, microfibres, silicone rubbers.

In the many videos on Iris van Herpen's website, the progress towards increasing fluidity and movement of the 3D-printed fabrics can easily be traced.[5] 'Voltage' (A/W 2013) features the first flexible 3D-printed dresses. The designs look like they have been struck and fractured by lightning as the familiar folds and loops are shattered and point outwards as ever-moving spikes or tentacles. In 'Wilderness Embodied' a year later (A/W 2014), the 3D-printed silicone actually looks like soft feathers. And yet another year later, in 'Biopiracy' (A/W 2015), the garments are semi-detached and flowing around the bodies of the models.

Yet, not all intricate folds are 3D printed. A dramatic coral-like structure can be found draped for a dress made of silver satin, for which van Herpen has applied various hand-plissé techniques in contrast to mechanically folded plissé ('Crystallization', A/W 2010).[6] Sophisticated craftsmanship does a superb job here. The design may be less technologically enhanced; nonetheless, the effect is an organic coral-like form of interlaced folds. Moreover, it may be significant to note another material effect of this design, namely the metal thread: the silver yarn makes this dress incredibly heavy. When I visited the archive of the Centraal Museum and was allowed to lift the dress out of its box, I just couldn't believe how much it weighed; the curator Ninke Bloemberg estimated it at 10 to 12 kilos. I was left to wonder how the ethereal effect of those neo-baroque folds could be prompted by such tangible materiality.

To return to the folds themselves, let me look at the collection 'Seijaku' A/W 2016 (Figure 3.1), which, according to information available on her website, is a Japanese concept for finding serenity amidst life's chaos.[7] Here we can see again the most complex layers of folds executed in the strangest of fabrics. The vision that sustains it is as conceptually ambitious as it is methodologically rigorous. Iris van Herpen writes that this collection 'visualises sound waves as evolving geometric

Figure 3.1 Iris van Herpen, collection 'Seijaku', A/W 2016. Look 1 on the catwalk show. The dress is formed from semi-transparent beige-orange-green acrylic strips in pastel colours that have been hand- and laser-cut and mounted onto a tulle ground to create intricate folds. The dress fastens down centre back with a long metal zip. © Team Peter Stigter.

patterns'.[8] To achieve that effect, she used mixed techniques that can but do not always include 3D printing: from traditional pleats to laser-cut polyurethane, and Swarovski crystals cast in transparent silicone, as well as handmade Shibori techniques and computer-3D-sculpted smocked techniques made up of hundreds of layers. On her website, van Herpen describes the complex ways in which she has created the fabrics for 'Seijaku': She has coated thousands of hand-blown glass bubbles in transparent silicone, creating a 'bioluminescent prism around the body'.[9] She has used a similar technique to silicone-coat tens of thousands of Swarovski crystals, creating a dress with 'the look of a wet skin covered in dew drops'.[10] High-tech materials are transformed into layers of plastic lamellae, glass beads or transparent organza that are folded onto each other in otherworldly silhouettes. Other methodological techniques include stitching pearl-coated rubber fabric onto black tulle or laser cutting and stretching a dress over black wire to scroll around the body. She has also applied 'a 3-D moiré technique in which hand-plissé and line-printed organza is hand stitched on transparent tulle'.[11] Again, traditional craftsmanship meets high-tech, in a dizzying display of boundary-shifting inventiveness. Thus, Japanese organza is woven from microfibres, creating infinitesimal softness in fabrics: 'threads five times thinner than human hair', allowing the fabric to be moulded with the traditional Shibori technique of folding, binding and wrapping.[12] Elsewhere, she describes how 3D printing enables her to create the finest detail up to ten lines a millimetre.[13] Already in earlier work ('Micro' collection, S/S 2012), she has used laser cutting of acrylic strips to create a plissé style: 'I love using non-traditional materials to evoke traditional techniques.'[14]

Therefore, the more advanced the techniques that Iris van Herpen experiments with, the more important the craftsmanship of the designing process. For example, in 'Lucid' (S/S 2016), she made dresses in collaboration with the artist and architect Philip Beesley, 'from transparent hexagonal laser-cut elements that are connected with translucent flexible tubes, creating a glistering bubble-like exoskeleton around the wearer's body'.[15] She again fused technology with handcraft for 'two 3-D printed Magma dresses that are combining flexible TPU printing, creating a fine web together with polyamide printing'.[16] She claims that one of the dresses is stitched from 5,000 3D-printed elements, creatively fusing silicone fibres, tubes and stitches. Scale and speed combine to shift the creative perspective. Furthermore, the temporal frame is also re-programmed by mixing old and quasi-forgotten crafting techniques with cutting-edge technological innovation and new materials. Through such daring interventions, van Herpen creates assemblages that subvert time barriers, linking the past with the future in a continuous present.

Take the 'Foliage Dress' from the collection 'Ludi Naturae' (S/S 2018, Latin for 'games of nature'), which she developed with scientists and researchers from the Delft University of Technology. On her website it reads: 'Leaf-like patterns are 3D printed as thin as 0.8 mm and tulle is laid into the 3D printer to print directly onto the fabric.'[17] The company Stratasys laid the fabric of the 'Foliage dress' into a 3D printer using PolyJet technology to print different materials simultaneously.[18] In the video by Ryan McDaniels, one can see that the 'Foliage dress' has achieved exceptional softness, but also how much of that process is still done by hand.[19]

Let me move to a rather spectacular dress from the collection 'Sympoiesis' (look 1, A/W 2025; see Figure 3.2). The Greek term 'sympoiesis' means literally 'making-with' or 'becoming-with' and refers to a collaborative relationship between organisms; I will discuss the term in more detail in the next chapter. With the aesthetics of this dress, Iris van Herpen returns to one of her early designs, the 'Water Dress' (look 17, 'Capriole' 2011). Both dresses express and enact her desire to try and catch a wave of water, but where the 'Water Dress' is ethereal and transparent, this look is quite corporeal in its sheer volume. In this case, 'ivory silk is draped upside down onto wave-shaped casts and coated with a fine layer of resin, becoming a cresting wave held in suspension – just before the chaos of the rolling crash', it reads on the website.[20]

In both designs, the folds evoke a sense of excess through the baroque exuberance of their forms and waves. The use of advanced materials and pioneering new processes emphasise and enhance 'strong shapes and extraordinary silhouettes' that express the fusion of fashion and technology in all its futuristic and speculative splendour.[21] The capacious folds in Iris van Herpen's designs connote entanglements of the human body

Figure 3.2 Iris van Herpen, collection 'Sympoiesis', A/W 2025. Circular shapes and geometric patterns in Look 1 on the catwalk show. The dress is made of ivory silk draped upside down onto wave-shaped casts and coated with a fine layer of resin. © Photographer Gio Staiano.

with the non-human organic and inorganic elements of cloth, silicone, water or foliage. Or, as Laura Marks poetically writes in her philosophical musings on the fold: 'One fabric, with body on the outside, soul on the inside, pleated into a labyrinth, in which every being is a fold.'[22] It's time to move on to a philosophy of the fold.

The Vibrations of the Fold

Van Herpen's designs that I discussed above can be described as a posthuman aesthetics, in the way that they morph art, nature, fashion and technology, as I argued in the previous chapter. At regular intervals, Iris van Herpen tries to visualise a non-human phenomenon: sound waves, a splash of water or the flight of a bird. Accounting for them is what science is supposed to do, and van Herpen obliquely engages with the knowledge systems of physics, geometry, biology, mathematics. The way in which she uses her artistic sensibility as a sort of radar to guide her through the maze of scientific information is quite extraordinary. And what her gaze focuses on is the constant flows of waves, particles, atoms, biomes – their ceaseless activism. A phenomenon in nature is visualised in her designs to create a hybrid figure of human and non-human, which is perceived through ever-recurring and evolving folds – forever enfolding, unfolding, refolding. The fold is a point in a continuum of motion and encounters. The fact that for van Herpen movement is so important in her designs may explain the stylistic element of the fold in so much of her work. Iris van Herpen says: 'In a lot of my designs, I express the vibrational qualities of our bodies. [...] When I think of all the trillions of vibrations that happen simultaneously inside us, I feel overwhelmed.'[23] Capturing the circulation of elementary particles and waves emerges as the central challenge. And indeed, ever since she has introduced fluidity into her designs, 'her dresses come to life with the slightest movement of the body, creating a ballet of textures and materials, friction and shifts, colours and transparency', as curator Cloé Pitiot writes.[24]

Such vibrant movement can be linked to the notion of the fold as the philosopher Gilles Deleuze develops in his book *The Fold* (1993).[25] I will tease out three points from his philosophical approach: how the fold unravels matter as dynamic; how the movement of the fold points to emotion and affect; and how the fold opens up to a process of becoming.[26]

Deleuze unravels the material qualities of the fold as a continuous dialogue between inside and outside. Turn the fabric of a dress this way, and a fold shows the inside; turn it that way, and the fold shows its outside. As Giuliana Bruno writes: 'It is the very simplicity of the fold that entails its remarkable complexity.'[27] Similarly, the exuberant folds of van Herpen's fashion designs create surprising folding-ins and folding-outs. The fold doubles the outside as much as it doubles the inside; inside-out becomes outside-in and the other way around. What is in? What is out? What is in-between? The folds do not present a total or frontal view, but create intervals of small differences in curvature, shifting the boundary between inside and outside of a garment. They create a single curved surface. Dresses fold in both inward and outward directions, or as Deleuze puts it, the fold moves between the outside and the inside, expanding on either side: 'the fold is divided into folds, which are tucked inside and which spill onto the outside'.[28] There is thus always an exteriority on the outside, and an interiority on the inside, which can swap places in the folds of van Herpen's fashion. It is in this perennial process of moving in-between inside and outside that the fold expresses its unlimited freedom. The fold is a way of thinking space and time as intertwined, as a dynamic relation, folded upon one another. By understanding space as a fold, there is no longer an absolute inside or outside: the infinite fold has '[...] an exterior always on the outside, an interior always on the inside', muses Deleuze.[29]

The asymmetrical and multilayered folds and foldings point to a state of flux where everything flows, not in a chaotic manner, but within the curving edge of a continuous surface or wave. Matter is a texture, writes Deleuze, a fabric, and all matter 'generally always tends to unfold its pleats at great length'.[30] Looking at any of van Herpen's designs one can see how the folds are dynamic, with a dispersion of a central line, opening up to a multiplicity of lines, notches, gaps, holes and fissures. These kinds of designs are fluid and constantly moving. Laura Marks explains that this kind of 'enfolding-unfolding aesthetics' connotes an entanglement that connects us to the world.[31]

The second point that I tease out of Deleuze's philosophy of the fold is its deep intensity. To be sure, there is a sensual delight in the pleats and creases of fabric, in the abundant, rising and falling folds of futuristic materials. In fashion, the fold is engaged in a game of concealing and revealing the body-in-motion. Here it is interesting to note that in art history, the fold is traditionally connected to the expression of emotion. Already in 1436, Leon Battista Alberti described in his short treatise *On Painting* how the folds of drapery, gowns and dresses indicate not only movement and the display of mastery over the materiality of paint, wood or marble but also that the folds, pleats and drapes create a sphere of agitation, drama, sensation and the expression of pure emotion.[32] The play of pathos is most prominently put forward in the quintessence of Baroque art: Bernini's sculptures. His sculpted draperies were typical of the Baroque and indeed helped shape the Baroque, creating an illusion of violent movement. The folds acquire a life of their own, quite independent of the human figure that they cover. As Anne Hollander wryly remarks of folds and draperies in paintings: 'It had become a potential manifestation more similar to unusual turbulence in the heavens than to household linen [...]'[33] And indeed, looking at Bernini's sculptures, there is not only a sensual delight in the pleats and creases of the cloth, but the abundant, rising and falling folds seem to flow with deep intensity. Similarly, in Iris van Herpen's look 1 of 'Sympoiesis', the folds of the dress seem to be alive with an intensity of their own. But take also another look, from the collection 'Sensory

Seas' (S/S 2020); on the website, you can see how the dress flows and moves around the model, 'blooming aquatically with each movement' like the ebb and flow of the sea (Figure 3.3).[34]

The white dress of Figure 3.3 looks complicated, and indeed, the description on the website is rather daunting: 'The 3D twisted vortex models were created in Rhino software, to then be cut on the KERN lasercutter with a triangulated grid of chevron-holes, which were put together in processes of lofting, slicing and nesting. Each layer was embellished by hand with a grid of minuscule transparent chevrons, creating vibrant coral textures that expand and contract around the body.'[35]

The folds of the dress show a garment in motion. Giuliana Bruno has pointed to the quality of motion as emotion in clothes: 'Home of the fold, fashion resides with the reversible continuity that, rather than separating, provides a breathing membrane – a skin – to the world. Sensorially speaking, clothes come alive in (e)motion.'[36] Note how the word emotion has the word 'motion' in it: something moves us, literally, emotionally. Iris van Herpen's fashion is a play of pathos – both passion and traction combined in embracing the vitality of matter. The motion of the clothes paradoxically grounds the flesh, but also suggests an idea of the body as incorporeal, a body of passions, affect and intensity. Van Herpen's folds of fashion express new pathways towards affect and intensity: 'The folds of clothing acquire an autonomy and a fullness that are not simply decorative effects. They convey the intensity of a spiritual force exerted on the body, either to turn it upside down or to stand or raise it up over

Figure 3.3 Iris van Herpen, collection 'Sensory Seas', S/S 2020. Look 19: intricate beehive-like layered folds in a dress made of white organza. © Photographer David Uzochukwu.

and again, but in every event to turn it inside out and to mold its inner surfaces', writes Deleuze.[37]

The affect of van Herpen's designs lies in the vertiginous loops of those entangled folds as they keep moving and affecting us – folding in, folding out, folding open. Dancing in time and space. They also seem to flow with deepening intensity. With life itself. This is where we get to the third point that I distil from Deleuze's philosophy of the fold: the process of becoming. Insofar as matter can fold, he writes, it is capable of becoming.[38] The fold involves a process of opening out to the world. This particular aspect of van Herpen's design signature of the fold shows the potentiality of a process of becoming, that is, of change and transformation. 'Becoming is a verb', writes Gilles Deleuze together with psychoanalyst Félix Guattari in their famed book *A Thousand Plateaus*.[39] This understanding of becoming is a dynamic process: by experimenting and looking for new ways of becoming, one can move beyond the fixed and confined self, the ego-centred entity that is the 'organised, signified, subjected' self that society demands of us.[40] The process of becoming understands the self as grounded and relational – as an eco-centric rather than an ego-centric entity. But also as a self that can change and transform. As Rosi Braidotti writes, one is grounded but can still flow.[41] Becoming means to move in a network of multiple relations, to set desires flowing by connecting to others – animals, plants, machines, molecules. It involves forming alliances with different affects, forces and intensities of life.

Iris van Herpen loves '[…] the creative process and becoming – of making matter come into existence […]', as Ariane Koek writes of 'Sensory Seas' (S/S 2020) in the catalogue *Sculpting the Senses*.[42] We can see that creative process in her collections, for example, becoming-animal in the supernatural laser-cut silicone feathers in her collection 'Voltage' (S/S 2013), or becoming-plant in the spores of mycelium in 'Roots of Rebirth' (S/S 2021). We see a becoming-organic in 'Hybrid Holism' (A/W 2012) and 'Earthrise' (A/W 2021), in which the high-tech designs look like coral reefs or swarms of insects or flocks of birds. As we saw above, she succeeds in catching a wave of water in a tangible form in 'Sympoeisis', but we can also witness a becoming-water in 'Sensory Seas' (S/S 2020). In the short film for the collection 'Carte Blanche' (S/S 2023), the models dance under water, becoming dreamy Melusines, female water spirits.[43] Two years earlier, a short film showed Domitille Kiger, a world-champion skydiver, actually jumping from a plane wearing a gown from the 'Earthrise' collection (A/W 2021).[44] Earthrise is the title of the photo in colour that astronaut William Anders made in 1968 of the planet Earth rising as seen from the lunar orbit – a picture that forever changed how humankind sees the Earth: beautiful and vulnerable, floating in black space. From the mycelium under the ground to swimming in the deep sea or flying in the high skies, van Herpen's designs are about becoming-other through symbiosis with nature, the body and technology.

Deleuze's idea that the fold is a way to think of identity as a process of becoming also circulates within a posthuman context, where the notion of becoming as a dynamic process rather than a fixed state of being is equally relevant.[45] The point here is that the experience of being affected by Iris van Herpen's folds is intimately connected to the sense of becoming that her posthuman aesthetics entails. This relation between affect and becoming has been made explicit by the posthuman idea that all that is alive is in a constant flux, driven by the generative force of affect as a potential for becoming. The multiple layers of fold upon fold show the posthuman design in all its dynamic force. In connecting with the body in ways that are not static, rigid or normalised, van Herpen's designs open up possibilities to slowly morph and transform. Iris van Herpen's experimental designs can be seen as an invitation to engage the viewer or wearer in a creative process of becoming, by transforming the body and going with the flow of the movement of the folds. The non-linear folds fold in and open within folds folding in and open within folds etcetera. Her 3D-printed designs create a play of multiple becomings, showing a path to flexibility in a complex world that is changing rapidly. As she says herself, 'We will have multiple identities in our near future.'[46]

Most impressive in the last few years is the sense of fluidity, dynamic energy and shifting patterns in van Herpen's designs. 'Meta Morphism' (A/W 2022) was, as the title indicates, inspired by Ovid's *Metamorphoses* and its themes of transformation. But also in the other collections, like 'Carte Blanche' (S/S

2023), 'Architectonics' (A/W 2023), 'Hybrid Show' (A/W 2024) and 'Sympoiesis' (A/W 2025), flowing dresses show the familiar billowing folds in PETG bubbles, dendrites of lace or voluminous clouds of organza. The fractal folds and distorted perspectives of these designs redefine fashion's traditional boundaries by vibrating around the body. This indicates that the process of becoming is about perpetual change and transformation. A process of becoming implies constant movement and transformation, and in that sense Deleuze and Guattari foreground the vibrancy of matter and the dynamics of time. Van Herpen's designs show that becoming is an ongoing process of change – one that unfolds through continuous metamorphosis. The process of becoming thus means to move beyond the static nature of matter and the dynamic nature of time; with each step, a dress by Iris van Herpen reveals '[…] a constant metamorphosis and fluctuation in space and time'.[47]

The labyrinths of ripples, loops, folds, waves, twists, pleats, wrinkles and circles in van Herpen's baroque designs make materials move, swing and sway. In her experiments with form, matter and time, she calls for a different relation to the body. The unstoppable movement points to ways of reinventing identity. Morphing new silhouettes, Iris van Herpen invites the wearer to inhabit the freedom of co-creating the body as new shapes. Her designs function as interfaces between inside and outside, depth and surface, deep-sea diving and skydiving, engaging the wearer in a creative process of becoming, transforming the body and reinventing the self. In creating folds, rhizomes and entanglements, van Herpen's voluminous designs open up an understanding of life as an infinite play of becoming – a dance of materials.[48]

Out of innovative technologies, new materials and assiduous craftsmanship, Iris van Herpen creates a new visual and material language to express the affective mood of a posthuman world. She thus demands a shift in our patterns of perception. These slightly alien, at times frightening, but often delicately beautiful designs take the human figure away from the conventional centre of attention, relocating the human to a knot in an interlaced network of organic and technological actors like pins and needles as well as codes and pixels. I have related the affect that van Herpen's folds have – an affect of beauty, of wonder, of strangeness – to the notion of becoming that her posthuman aesthetics enable. The folds show Iris van Herpen to be an artist who succeeds in transforming her futuristic visions into material, technologically mediated and intensely posthuman designs.

As I have argued in this chapter, the fold is dynamic, constantly vibrating. As a curvature of space and a non-hierarchical framing of time, the fold is just light, colour, depth, surface, shape. The folds and pleats of van Herpen's designs are in the words of Deleuze 'at once continuous, mobile, and fluttering'.[49] The vibrations of those folds indicate an expansive movement, a line of flight, which opens us up to a spiraling process of creative becoming. The fold of fashion then is a dynamic process of becoming multiple, of searching for a new place of the posthuman being in the world. Fashioning the fold can help to envisage a process of becoming, where we humans continue to fold, enfold, unfold and refold. In the next chapter I will show how not only humans, but the whole of the natural world participates in that process of folding, enfolding, unfolding and refolding.

Notes

1 Kellina Moore, 'Designing for a Pop Star'. *The New York Times*, 17 April 2026. https://www.nytimes.com/2026/04/17/style/mother-mary-costumes-iris-van-herpen.html?smid=url-share.
2 Ibid.
3 Bradley Quinn, *Textile Futures. Fashion, Design and Technology*. (Oxford: Berg, 2010); Andrew Bolton, *Manus x Machina: Fashion in an Age of Technology*. (New York: The Metropolitan Museum of Art, 2016).
4 Ninke Bloemberg (ed.), *Het Nieuwe Ambacht: Iris van Herpen en haar inspiratie* ['The New Craft: Iris van Herpen and Her Inspiration']. (Utrecht: Centraal Museum, 2011), 41, my translation.
5 https://www.irisvanherpen.com/.
6 On Iris van Herpen's website, the collection of 'Crystallization' has been integrated in 'Capriole', which was Iris van Herpen's first haute couture show in Paris in 2011. The dress is difficult to find on the website: It is the last design in the black and white 'Discover the editorial' of 'Capriole', A/W 2011. https://www.irisvanherpen.com/collections/capriole/editorial-14. Note that the exaggerated skirt of look 8 is another example of complicated folds that are not 3D printed.
7 https://www.irisvanherpen.com/collections/seijaku.
8 Ibid.
9 Ibid.
10 Ibid.
11 Ibid.

12 Ibid.
13 Quoted in Bolton, *Manus x Machina*, xvii.
14 Bolton, *Manus x Machina*, xx.
15 https://www.irisvanherpen.com/collections/lucid/lucid-molly-sj-lowe.
16 Ibid.
17 https://www.irisvanherpen.com/collections/ludi-naturae/ludi-naturae-photography-by-molly-sj-lowe.
18 See the website of 3DFashion by Stratasys: https://3dprintedart.stratasys.com/fashion/project-one-tg5ld-c24df-gzm69-wam56-r8zsy.
19 https://www.irisvanherpen.com/collections/ludi-naturae.
20 https://www.irisvanherpen.com/collections/sympoiesis/about-18.
21 Bradley Quinn, *Fashion Futures*. (London: Merrell, 2012), 12.
22 Laura U. Marks, *The Fold: From Your Body to the Cosmos*. (Durham: Duke University Press, 2024), 28.
23 Hans Ulrich Obrist, 'Interview with Iris van Herpen' in Catalogue *Iris van Herpen: Sculpting the Senses*. (Amsterdam: Lannoo, 2023), 29.
24 Cloé Pitiot, in Catalogue *Iris van Herpen: Sculpting the Senses*. (Amsterdam: Lannoo, 2023), 17.
25 Gilles Deleuze, *The Fold: Leibniz and the Baroque*, trans. T. Conley. (Minneapolis: University of Minnesota Press, 1993 (1988)).
26 I have written extensively about the fold in fashion; Anneke Smelik, 'Fashioning the Fold: Multiple Becomings' in *The Deleuzian Century: Art, Activism, Society*, ed. Rosi Braidotti and Rick Dolphijn. (Amsterdam: Brill Rodopi, 2014), 37–55; and Anneke Smelik, 'Gilles Deleuze: Bodies-without-Organs in the Folds of Fashion' in *Thinking through Fashion. A Guide to Key Theorists*, 2nd ed., ed. Agnès Rocamora and Anneke Smelik. (London: Bloomsbury, 2025), 175–188.
27 Giuliana Bruno, 'Pleats of Matter, Folds of the Soul' in *Afterimages of Gilles Deleuze's Film Philosophy*, ed. David Rodowick. (Minneapolis: University of Minnesota Press, 2010), 222.
28 Deleuze, *The Fold*, 35.
29 Ibid.
30 Ibid., 143.

31 Marks, *The Fold*, 34.
32 Leon Battista Alberti, *On Painting (Della pittura)*, trans. John Spencer. (New Haven: Yale University Press, 1966 [1435–1436]), 81.
33 Anne Hollander, *Seeing Through Clothes*. (London: Penguin, 1988), 5.
34 Description of 'Sensory Seas' by Iris van Herpen: https://www.irisvanherpen.com/collections/sensory-seas/sensory-seas-photography-by-molly-sj-lowe.
35 Ibid.
36 Bruno, 'Pleats of Matter, Folds of the Soul', 225.
37 Deleuze, *The Fold*, 122.
38 Ibid., 37.
39 Gilles Deleuze and Félix Guattari, *A Thousand Plateaus: Capitalism and Schizophrenia*, trans. Brian Massumi. (Minneapolis: University of Minnesota Press, 1987), 239.
40 Deleuze and Guattari, *A Thousand Plateaus*, 161.
41 Rosi Braidotti, *Posthuman Feminism*. (Cambridge: Polity Press, 2022), 141.
42 Ariane Koek, 'On the Edge of the Im/Material' in Catalogue *Iris van Herpen: Sculpting the Senses*. (Amsterdam: Lannoo, 2023), 235.
43 Video 'Carte Blanche', Julie Gautier & Iris van Herpen, 4 min 17 sec, 2023. https://www.irisvanherpen.com/collections/carte-blanche.
44 Video 'Earthrise', Masha Vasyukova, Art + Commerce, 6 min 36 sec, 2021. https://www.irisvanherpen.com/collections/earthrise.
45 Rosi Braidotti, *The Posthuman*. (Cambridge: Polity Press, 2013).
46 Quoted in Obrist, 'Interview with Iris van Herpen', 33.
47 Koek, 'On the Edge of the Im/Material', 234.
48 Anneke Smelik, 'A Dance of Materials: Between the Organic and Inorganic in Iris van Herpen's Fashion'. *National Gallery of Victoria Art Journal*, Australia, 11 December 2023.
49 Deleuze, *The Fold*, 124.

Chapter 4

A LIVING DRESS

In this chapter, I explore one of van Herpen's primary sources of inspiration: the natural world. Her designs draw on phenomena such as water, smoke, mycelium and the subtle motion of bird wings, moving across both microscopic and cosmic dimensions. In 2025 she started beekeeping, fascinated by how a bee colony functions. I argue that her broad conception of nature also shapes her approach to sustainability. Central to the chapter is the 'living dress', a striking work that exemplifies van Herpen's design philosophy by incorporating living systems into fashion and reimagining the relationship between clothing and life itself.

'It's Alive! Iris Van Herpen's Latest Innovation? A Dress Made From 125 Million Bioluminescent Algae' cheered *Vogue.*[1] A 'first-of-its-kind living look', wrote *Dezeen.*[2] And *Nature* exclaimed 'Science on the catwalk: Iris van Herpen gives gowns a glow up'.[3] Once again, Iris van Herpen had hit the headlines with a novel experiment, from fashion magazines like *Vogue* to science journals like *Nature*. What was the excitement all about?

The enthusiasm concerned the dress with which Iris van Herpen opened her collection 'Sympoiesis' (A/W 2025; see Figure 4.1). It was a dress made from 125 million bioluminescent algae, the so-called Pyrocystis lunula, that emit light in response to movement. I saw the dress in the exhibition *Sculpting the Senses* in museum Kunsthal in Rotterdam in 2026, where it was exhibited in a glass cage, carefully kept alive in the just mix of water and air at the right temperature. Or, as Iris van Herpen's website puts it: The dress is 'attentively cared for in conditions to mimic their natural marine home, with humidity, temperature, and circadian rhythm all tuned to their precise needs'.[4] On the video next to the exhibited dress, you could see how it gives off light when it is worn in the dark on the catwalk.

Fashion designer Iris van Herpen had worked with biodesigner Chris Bellamy to create this dress. The website details how the algae were grown in seawater baths with a nutrient gel over several months, before being moulded into a protected membrane and embedded into the dress. Strictly speaking, the dress was not so much designed or constructed, but grown by hydro-culture, that is to say, generated by a careful combination of nature and culture. As the fashion house explains: 'Caring for the garment, and for the 125 million Pyrocystis lunula it contains, requires a symbiotic relationship and redefines the creation traditions entirely, as the garment is cultivated rather than constructed.'[5]

Figure 4.1 Iris van Herpen, collection 'Sympoiesis', A/W 2025. The blue 'Living Dress', made from 125 million bioluminescent algae, the Pyrocystis lunula, that emit light in response to movement. © Photographer Gio Staiano.

A year later, in 2026, Iris van Herpen was selected as the first recipient of the inaugural Perrier-Jouët Design for Nature Award, presented in collaboration with Design Miami. The new award recognises designers whose work bridges artistic innovation with ecological consciousness. The designation of the award is somewhat misleading, as 'Nature' is not the only component at play in what van Herpen designs here. Rooted in the spirit of Art Nouveau and its celebration of the deep interconnectedness between nature, culture and creativity, the Design for Nature Award invited van Herpen to propose regenerative pathways for the future of design.[6] She was granted carte blanche to create a singular work that debuted at Design Miami in 2026.

In the previous chapters, I have expanded on van Herpen's ongoing exploration at the intersection of innovative technology and artisanal craftsmanship in the past two decades. However, I have not yet focused on the other important source of inspiration for van Herpen: that complex self-organising living system we call nature. 'Nature has always been my main source of inspiration', says van Herpen, 'and I felt I could come closer to nature by embracing technology'.[7] The Perrier-Jouët Design for Nature Award 'encourages projects that merge artistic innovation with environmental responsibility, fostering collaborative and regenerative design practices that embody a constructive optimism for a more sustainable future'.[8] The question for this chapter is how van Herpen has responded to the quest for sustainability in the field of fashion. I want to focus on the extent to which she shifted the boundaries of the continuum nature–culture, with the aid of technologies but guided by her own aesthetic vision.

Biodesign

'Sustainability' literally means: to sustain, to maintain, to endure, in both space and time. The question is what exactly needs to be sustained? More specifically, the question is what needs to be sustained within what is called the Anthropocene – the geological epoch defined by the negative human impact on the planet's ecosystems. Generally, it refers to sustaining the planet Earth in such a way that it can feed the eco-sphere, flora and fauna, of which humankind is an integral part. This means that the familiar lifestyle, the specific economic system we inhabit and the political organisations that govern us, may no longer be sustainable: consumerism, capitalism or market-driven neoliberalism need to be critically assessed. Their shortcomings have become dramatically visible.

The fashion system, and especially fast fashion, is a line of flow that cuts across all three dimensions. It is considered a highly capitalist enterprise because of its push for a very fast turnover of goods.[9] But it is also a crucial element in identity formation and sense of selfhood; and freedom of choice is, of course, a pillar of democratic political systems. For the fashion system to change and improve, therefore, a great deal needs to happen.

There are at least two different axes to tackle: both social and environmental sustainability. By now, most consumers know that the system of fast fashion is cracking at the seams because of overlapping axes of injustice. On the environmental front, we witness the depletion of natural resources, pollution of earth and water and the ever-cumulating heaps of discarded garments. On the social level, we see the tremendous financial power of brands and the ruthless exploitation of garment workers – mostly women – especially in the Global South. Clearly, environmental degradation cannot be disconnected from the human exploitation in the labour market. In that sense, transnational capitalism is responsible for the persistent inequalities and injustices of the fashion system – for ecological as well as social oppression. The fast fashion system is quite rightly criticised from many quarters for its dire impact on the climate crisis and on social and economic justice.

Maison Iris van Herpen does not produce fast fashion nor mass-produced clothes for cheap consumption. Far from it, it creates artisanal couture with a high-tech edge. It is therefore fair to say that as a designer, the creator of the fashion brand (if you can even call it that) is not part of the objectionable fast fashion system. It is, from conception, by its very nature and by the protocols of its execution, purely 'slow fashion'.[10] Loud statements and political manifestos are not in the style of van Herpen. While 'Van Herpen does not overtly critique the state of global environmental politics, it is hard to read her work separately from conversations of the Anthropocene', as Vanessa

Gerrie astutely claims.[11] Van Herpen not only integrates art, technology and science but also 'links the earth's natural phenomena with that of the human experience'.[12] Her fashion designs touch upon both the social and the environmental ecologies I mentioned above, and can thus provoke empathy and understanding for our relationship with nature. Thus, the ethical drive runs deep and broad in her design. According to curator Louise Curtis, Iris van Herpen is indeed driven 'by a desire for synergy with nature' and she has therefore 'shifted the focus of her research towards current ecological urgencies, with a view to highlighting the fragility of the environment and our future world'.[13] Nature is both a fragile environment to take care of and a source of inspiration to study attentively, so much is clear from the descriptions of her collections on her website. Whether it is water, smoke, mycelium of mushrooms or the fluttering wings of a bird in flight, van Herpen is intrigued by the mysteries of earth, sky and the deep ocean and tries to translate them into her fashion designs. From the infinitesimally small to the immeasurably large, she has a fascination for the cosmos, write curators Cloé Pitiot and Louise Curtis.[14] I would go further and argue that it is rather in a holistic framework that we should situate van Herpen's view on the intertwined effects of social and environmental sustainability.

Yet, activism is not too far off, but it is done with discretion and respect. Maison Iris van Herpen has actually developed concrete sustainable alternatives, mostly in the field of new nature–cultural materials. For example, for her collections

'Earthrise' (A/W 2021) and 'Roots of Rebirth' (S/S 2021), she collaborated with Parley for the Oceans, a global environmental organisation that gives a second life to plastic waste recovered from the sea. Another example is her collection 'Meta Morphism' (A/W 2022), for which she developed biodegradable resources together with Eric Klarenbeek and Maartje Dros.[15] They had developed a new bio-technological method that enabled them to 3D-print organic substances, such as algae or mycelium. Using these processes, the three together created the 'Singularity Jumpsuit', made from recycled organza and cacao transformed into biopolymer filaments.[16] As Iris van Herpen recounts: 'In my designs, I often develop sustainable materials that reflect the natural worlds, such as banana-leaf fabrics, biodegradable plastics and cacao-bean prints.'[17] They reflect what was the natural order, but also transcend it, by reworking it through technology, thus ascending to an altogether different plane of creative activity. By operating such radically different choices, van Herpen is – at times – replacing classical materials of fashion: animal skins, wool, water-intensive cotton and other plantation fibres, but also synthetic, fossil fuel-based fabrics that are all petrol derivatives. This alone is a revolutionary gesture, albeit still in small measures.

Biodesign means experimenting with biology – living matter – outside a scientific laboratory. Moreover, the term 'biodesign' is not necessarily reserved for fashion; on the contrary, it covers a range of practices – from architecture and industrial design to fine arts and medicine.[18] In the case of fashion, biodesign usually refers to the generation of fabrics made of new recycled organic fibres, for example made of orange skin, coffee waste or from mycelium of mushrooms. In addition, biology-inspired approaches to design are not necessarily new.[19] To mention here some well-known examples in the field of fashion: In 2003 Suzanne Lee invented the word BioCouture for her project of growing fabrics from plant cells like kombucha. She is now the CEO of Biofabricate,[20] which develops new materials and products with and through biological matter. Another early example of biodesign includes the Tissue Culture and Art project, for which Oron Catts and Ionat Zurr developed 'victimless leather' in 2004 in an experiment using human and non-human cells to grow a jacket.[21] A third early example concerns Helen Storey's Wonderland project for which she, together with scientist Tony Ryan, developed biodegradable plastic to find sustainable solutions to the problem of waste in the fashion industry. In 2008, Nick Knight made a film *Wonderland* as a conclusion to the project.[22] Storey has donated her archive to the University of the Arts in London in 2024.[23]

More recently, mycelium fibres of mushrooms have been used to produce vegan leather, for example Mylo, by Bolt Threads in the United States, who made fabrics for Stella McCartney and Balenciaga in 2021 and 2022. Mycelium is also used for producing sustainable fabrics by Mycotex, Neffa, in the Netherlands. Other examples are fabrics made from seaweed, for example by Tabinotabi in Venice, Italy. There are many other examples of fabrics made from cellulose materials other than cotton or linen, for example, nettles, orange skin, pineapple skin and even fish scales.

To come back to Maison Iris van Herpen; the embrace of biology to create new technological processes is then not necessarily new as a technique, but in her case, it always results in eerily beautiful designs. Not so long ago, she said that she was fascinated but: 'I'm a little scared of biotechnology because of its possible uses in social engineering. I do see a lot of potential, however, in materiality.'[24] Her fascination for exploring biotechnology got the upper hand: 'If you look at biology, it's a hundred times more complex than technology. So where biology and technology come together is fascinating.'[25] Van Herpen's artistic flair is the gamechanger. Let me highlight a few collections that are inspired by nature rather than biodesign in the strict sense of the word. If any fashion designer systematically addresses the relationship between 'nature' and 'the machine', it is Iris van Herpen: her collections acknowledge the convergence of biology with technology. Take, for example, the collection 'Syntopia' (A/W 2018), for which van Herpen tried to capture the overlapping of feathers together with the movement of bird wings in flight – ephemeral and quivering (Figure 4.2). Watching a model walk in the 'Frozen Falls' dress and headpiece is an amazing experience.[26] The dress dances around the body while the face is covered in shimmering shades of pale blue. As always, movement – the dance of materials – is so important for the spectacular designs of van Herpen, herself a trained dancer. In this case, the wavering phenomenon

Figure 4.2 Iris van Herpen, collection 'Syntopia', A/W 2018. Look 19, the 'Frozen Falls' dress and headpiece as shown at the exhibition *Sculpting the Senses* (Paris, 2023). Made of silk (organza, tulle), cotton and polyester. © Photo Anneke Smelik.

of nature is designed as a material dress that is laser-cut from Mylar and white cotton heat-bonded to hundreds of layers of two-toned dyed blue organza. As van Herpen recounts on her website:

> As a former dancer, the transformation within movement has hypnotised me. For this collection I looked closely at the minutiae of bird flight and the intricate echoing forms within avian motion. The artists Studio Drift and the scientist Etienne Jules Marey inspired me to look more closely at the draping of a garment through chronophotography. By slowing down time into split seconds I started breaking down the usual draping of fabric, to then layer the milliseconds all slightly shifted, like the layering of a bird's feather.[27]

Here the fold – the curving of space and time – re-enters the conversation. Pleating and laser cutting, the result of van Herpen's design process of digitally designed weaving, creates thousands of transparent folds 'that drape like time-lapse motion'.[28] The image of the dress shows the lines of those folds waving between the now (the 'falls') and time immemorial (the 'frozen'). The 'Frozen Falls' dress and headpiece signpost a continuum between nature and the machine, or between the human and the non-human, the material and the immaterial, and also between the deep time of geology and the dynamic time of genealogy and history. The dress may be inspired by nature – the fluttering movement of bird wings – but its folds are highly technologically mediated in the making of its fabric and in the artificial shapes that it approximates. Truly magical to see and profoundly rigorous.

For the collection 'Sensory Seas' (S/S 2020) Iris van Herpen used metamaterials to mirror the central nervous systems of branched deep-sea organisms, called Hydrozoa: 'Shifting between a polypoid stage and a medusa stage, the Hydrozoa embroider the oceans like aqueous fabrics, forming layers of living lace.'[29] In a form of biomimicry, the garments simulate marine organisms, exploring geometric patterns derived from microscopic organisms. She worked again with architect and designer Philip Beesley, one of her preferred collaborators. Vanessa Gerrie quite rightly observes that van Herpen creates wearable garments that are inspired by *unseen* natural phenomena: 'her practice brings scientific data and natural phenomena to life in material aesthetic form'.[30] It may be opportune to quote van Herpen's website to read the rather baffling technological language:

> 3D twisted vortex models were created in Rhino software, numbered and sliced into 3mm distance, to then be cut on the KERN lasercutter with a triangulated grid of chevron-holes. Grasshopper scripts smoothened the processes of lofting, slicing and nesting. Each layer was embellished by hand with a grid of minuscule transparent chevrons,

> creating vibrant coral textures that expand and contract around the body.[31]

For the collection 'Roots of Rebirth' (S/S 2021), Iris van Herpen explored the interconnectedness of the human body and the natural world by weaving the enigmatic empire of mushrooms into her designs. Mimicking the fine threads of mycelium onto expandable lace enhanced with laser-cut organza, 3D and hand embroidery, the dresses form fractal networks that entwine the body, visualising 'the entanglement of life that breathes beneath our feet'.[32] Weaving a dialogue between fungi, the human body and technology, the designs become bodies-without-organs that move with a 'living lace of spores'.[33] The movement comes from the living and self-replicating power of the organic: the spores, fungi and all matter that go on living. Van Herpen replicates this energy through the inorganic by building interfaces and a shared habitat for the organic; each garment in the collection generating movement and performing a dance of materials.

In previous chapters, I have argued that hybridity is key to the figure of the posthuman because of the interconnections between the biological and the technological. So far, we have seen that van Herpen's collections are inspired by both: by biology and by technology. She merges the human (mostly female) body with animals, trees or plants ('Wilderness Embodied' A/W 2013; 'Biopiracy' A/W 2014), wisps of smoke ('Refinery Smoke' S/S 2009), sound waves ('Seijaku' A/W 2016), dendrites and synapses ('Sensory Seas' S/S 2020; 'Architectonics' A/W 2023) and much more. It is the hybridity that adds a self-organising energy to the designs. Nature is capable of dynamic self-organisation, but van Herpen shows that technology is too. Not only does nature live, but technology is also smart and alive, that is to say capable of self-organising. The contrast of producing organic structures with the latest technologies creates a posthuman aesthetic – an aesthetic that is post-naturalistic, built upon and enacting a nature–culture continuum.

Sympoiesis

It is time to come back to the 'living dress', famously made of 125 million bioluminescent algae, the Pyrocystis lunula, that emit light in response to movement. Myers (2022) defines biodesign as 'the incorporation of living organisms as essential components in design, enhancing the function of the finished work'.[34] That is exactly what the living dress does!

Let me further explore the meaning of the word 'sympoiesis', the title for van Herpen's A/W collection of 2025 for which the 'Living Dress' was created. Sympoiesis derives from the ancient Greek compound 'sún' ('with, together') and 'poíêsis' ('creation, production'), and it means 'making-with' or 'becoming-with'.[35] It describes a collaborative relationship between organisms that work together to create and maintain a shared ecosystem, emphasising the collective agency of multiple organisms in shaping their environment. It is closely related to the more familiar notion of symbiosis, which refers to a mutually beneficial relationship between two or more different species, where they rely on each other for survival and reproduction. Note how van Herpen speaks of 'a symbiotic relationship' between the garment and the algae in the quote above.

On her website, van Herpen does not explain the term sympoiesis, but writes that she is worried about 'the growing fragility' of the interdependence between 'the primordial rhythm of the organic and the human imperative of the technological'.[36] With the collection 'Sympoiesis' she wishes to create a collaboration with nature itself: 'In this time of ecological emergency and biodiversity loss, biodesign invites us to rethink the way we 'use' materials, to visualise a future where all human design is not just inspired by nature, but integrated with it', says van Herpen. 'It highlights the interdependence between humans and nature, viewing the body not as isolated, but as an ecosystem – where fashion becomes alive, responsive, and deeply connected with the natural world.'

Van Herpen refers in her editorial of 'Sympoiesis' to the Gaia thesis of James Lovelock, but the idea of sympoiesis has mostly been developed by the biologist Lynn Margulis, who co-authored many articles with Lovelock. In fact, it was she that suggested the term 'sympoiesis' for a new view of evolution, not one of selfish genes, but of 'the intimacy of strangers', her phrase to indicate the idea of generative enfolding of bacteria, critters, microbes and all kinds of single-celled organisms in a process of 'becoming-with each other', as Donna Haraway calls it.[37] Together Lovelock and Margulis suggested 'The Gaia

Hypothesis' in 1974, proposing the idea that the Earth and its biological systems function as a single entity, regulated by self-correcting feedback loops that maintain conditions favourable for life.[38] This idea is quite accepted today but was highly controversial when Lovelock and Margulis introduced it in the 1970s.

As both the concepts of sympoiesis and symbiosis highlight the interconnectedness and interdependence of organisms, as well as their enduring vitality, they fit in perfectly with the central ideas of new materialism – that matter matters, and that matter has some kind of agency – as I discussed in Chapter 2. The living dress grown from algae, of Iris van Herpen's collection 'Sympoiesis' (A/W 2025), is almost an immediate illustration of the main tenet of new materialism: that matter is an emergent and dynamic flow that forever changes and transforms. As Iris van Herpen already said in 2014: 'Everything is connected. It is one organism.'[39] This is also one of the central ideas of Donna Haraway's thought.

The term sympoiesis has been made more widely known by Donna Haraway in her book *Staying with the Trouble*. She writes, 'it is a simple word; it means "making-with"'.[40] Haraway uses the idea of sympoiesis, making-with or becoming-with, to challenge individualistic, human-centred thinking. In the context of ecological crisis, she argues that we should think in terms of interdependence, not independence. To put it simply, nothing makes itself. All systems are collectively produced: organisms, ecosystems and even technologies emerge through ongoing interactions among many beings. This making-with, or becoming-with, is exactly what is happening in the construction, or rather, cultivation of Iris van Herpen's living dress. The dress was not created in the classical sense of a human designer making it, but it was grown by caring for the 125 million Pyrocystis lunula it contains. I recall that Iris van Herpen explained that to care for the garment, and for the algae, requires a mutual relationship – a process of sympoiesis.

We remember from earlier chapters that posthuman thought foregrounds relationships between the human and the non-human. Similarly, for Haraway, sympoiesis involves collaboration across species, humans, animals, microbes, plants, machines – or cyborgs in her terminology. She calls this open-ended process of forever becoming a 'practice of multispecies becoming-with'.[41] Boundaries are porous: There are no fully self-contained individuals, or algae or bacteria, or plants or animals; everything is entangled with others. Rather than focusing on human dominance as we know it in neoliberalism or more generally in Western culture, the idea is to focus on multispecies entanglements.

Haraway's book has made quite an impact in its call for ethical responsibility and to take care of a damaged Earth. It follows that if we are all entangled with one another, we should care for one another. In the context of the ecological crises, she asks 'to cultivate the capacity to respond, response-ability'.[42] Against the outrage of human exceptionalism, she suggests extending our accountability towards the non-human world. In the case of fashion, we should care for the fabrics, for the spillage of water in growing cotton, for the abuse of the workers in the factories, for the pollution of earth and water, and the waste dumped in the Global South. As consumers, we are responsible for overconsumption, while producers are responsible for overproduction. Haraway writes: 'We are all responsible to and for shaping conditions for multispecies flourishing in the face of terrible histories, but not in the same ways. The differences matter – in ecologies, economies, species, lives.'[43] If we look again at the quote from Iris van Herpen's website on the living dress, made of algae, it is interesting to see how much care they take of these living organisms, invisible to the human eye: The dress is 'attentively cared for in conditions to mimic their natural marine home, with humidity, temperature, and circadian rhythm all tuned to their precise needs'.[44] What is at play here are all the elements and entities of our atmosphere, hydrosphere, geosphere and biosphere. This holistic attitude is truly in concordance with Haraway's call for making multispecies flourish.

One living dress, made of algae, does not change the fashion system. As Iris van Herpen says in an interview: 'If you only use sustainable materials – which is wonderful – but produce in massive amounts, we still don't have enough sustainable resources.'[45] Yes, van Herpen confirms, we need to develop and use sustainable materials, but it is not enough considering the sheer volume of clothes produced in the world: 'we should show fewer collections and focus more on quality rather than quantity'.[46]

The living dress may not be the most beautiful garment that Iris van Herpen has designed, but it is surely one of the most moving and thought-provoking ones – vulnerable in its aliveness, it shines light in the darkness of our damaged Earth.

Notes

1 Amy Verner, 'It's Alive! Iris Van Herpen's Latest Innovation? A Dress Made From 125 Million Bioluminescent Algae'. *Vogue*, 6 July 2025. https://www.vogue.com/article/iris-van-herpen-living-dress-125-million-bioluminescent-algae.
2 Cajsa Carlson, 'Iris van Herpen Dress Covered in Glowing Algae is "Cultivated Rather than Constructed"'. *Dezeen Magazine*, 10 July 2025. https://www.dezeen.com/2025/07/10/glowing-algae-dress-iris-van-herpen/.
3 https://www.nature.com/immersive/d41586-025-02068-x/index.html.
4 https://www.irisvanherpen.com/collections/sympoiesis/about-18.
5 Ibid.
6 https://www.perrier-jouet.com/en-ww/design-for-nature-award.
7 Quoted in Hans Ulrich Obrist, 'Interview with Iris van Herpen' in Catalogue *Iris van Herpen: Sculpting the Senses*. (Amsterdam: Lannoo, 2023), 29.
8 Ibid.
9 Hazel Clark, *Slow*. (London: Bloomsbury Series 'Fashion in Action', 2026).
10 Ibid.
11 Vanessa Gerrie, *Borderless Fashion Practice: Contemporary Fashion in the Metamodern Age*. (New Brunswick: Rutgers University Press, 2023), 128.
12 Ibid.

13 Louise Curtis in Catalogue *Iris van Herpen: Sculpting the Senses.* (Amsterdam: Lannoo, 2023), 46.
14 Cloé Pitiot and Louise Curtis, in Catalogue *Iris van Herpen: Sculpting the Senses.* (Amsterdam: Lannoo, 2023), 200.
15 Curtis, Catalogue *Iris van Herpen: Sculpting the Senses*, 46.
16 Ibid.
17 Quoted in Obrist, Catalogue *Iris van Herpen: Sculpting the Senses*, 32.
18 William Myers, *Bio Design: Nature, Science, Creativity*, 3rd edn (London: Thames and Hudson, 2022).
19 Jessica Hemmings, 'Grown Fashion: Animal, Vegetable or Plastic?' *Textile: the Journal of Cloth & Culture* 6, no. 3 (2008): 262–273.
20 https://www.biofabricate.co/.
21 https://tcaproject.net/portfolio/victimless-leather/.
22 https://www.showstudio.com/projects/wonderland/.
23 https://www.arts.ac.uk/about-ual/press-office/stories/in-pictures-professor-helen-storey-rdi,-mbes-life-in-fashion.
24 Quoted in Andrew Bolton, *Manus x Machina: Fashion in an Age of Technology.* (New York: The Metropolitan Museum of Art, 2016), xix–xx.
25 Bolton, *Manus x Machina*, xix.
26 See the videos of Blitzkickers, 'Iris van Herpen ~ Syntopia'. YouTube, 2018. https://www.youtube.com/watch?v=xtGq1zpTDQo. And SHOWstudio, 'Watch Iris Van Herpen's Syntopia Couture Collection Come to Life'. YouTube, 2018. https://www.youtube.com/watch?v=GSTRyPWRJpw.
27 https://www.irisvanherpen.com/collections/syntopia/syntopia-photography-by-molly-sj-lowe.
28 Ibid.
29 https://www.irisvanherpen.com/collections/sensory-seas/sensory-seas-photography-by-molly-sj-lowe.
30 Gerrie, *Borderless Fashion Practice*, 122.
31 https://www.irisvanherpen.com/collections/sensory-seas/sensory-seas-photography-by-molly-sj-lowe.
32 https://www.irisvanherpen.com/collections/roots-of-rebirth/editorial-1.

33 Ibid.

34 Myers, *Bio Design*.

35 Nicoletta Isar, 'Sympoiesis', No year. https://artsandculturalstudies.ku.dk/research/art-and-earth/environmental-humanities-glossary/sympoiesis/.

36 https://www.irisvanherpen.com/collections/sympoiesis/editorial-23.

37 Donna Haraway, *Staying with the Trouble: Making Kin in the Chthulucene*. (Durham: Duke University Press, 2016), 60.

38 James Lovelock and Lynn Margulis, 'Atmospheric Homeostasis by and for the Biosphere: The Gaia Hypothesis'. *Tellus* 26, nos. 1–2 (1974): 2–10.

39 Iris van Herpen, *A Magazine Curated by Iris van Herpen*. No. A13. (Antwerp: A Publisher, 2014), 27. https://amagazinecuratedby.com/collection/iris-van-herpen/.

40 Haraway, *Staying with the Trouble*, 60.

41 Ibid., 78.

42 Ibid.

43 Ibid., 116.

44 https://www.irisvanherpen.com/collections/sympoiesis/about-18.

45 Quoted in Cajsa Carlos, 'Biodesign Adds "a Whole New Range of Possibilities" to Fashion Says Iris van Herpen'. *Dezeen Magazine*, 22 September 2025. https://www.dezeen.com/2025/09/25/biodesign-fashion-iris-van-herpen-interview/.

46 Ibid.

Chapter 5

DESIGNING FOR DANCE

In this chapter, I investigate van Herpen's engagement with the body and movement, an interest shaped by her training in classical ballet and contemporary dance. Motion lies at the core of her design philosophy, informing her work for dance, opera and theatrical productions. Creating garments for performance entails particular demands related to durability, visibility and freedom of movement. Her collaborations with choreographers have resulted in visually compelling yet at times constraining designs, including weighty dresses and tightly structured leather suits. These creations expose a tension between aesthetic experimentation and practical functionality. I will show how she increasingly turns towards light, flowing garments that deliberately explore notions of fluidity and flexible identity.

Throughout her career, Iris van Herpen has stressed the lasting influence that learning to dance has had on her design practice. In her youth, van Herpen trained for both classical ballet and modern dance. This training has made her highly attuned to the body and its potential for fluid movement:

> In my younger years, I wanted to be a dancer. The movement and control I learnt then are still essential to my way of working now. I still use that tension, that friction. I am always looking for control, but I prefer chaos. In my work control creates balance, but I prefer that which comes from chaos. I think it is chaos that has created life. The visionary people with whom I work within the spheres of physics and chemistry, sculpture, dance and architecture inspire me to think differently. They teach me how not to work in circles.[1]

It is therefore no surprise that Iris van Herpen has designed costumes for modern dance as well as for theatre companies, like many other fashion designers.[2] Fashion – especially on the catwalk – is, after all, closely related to theatrical performance. The key idea here is flowing motion. In both fashion and dance, expression and affect are conveyed through the language of the body. In spite of the repeated references that van Herpen makes in interviews and editorials to her childhood training and experience as a dancer, and to her fascination with movement, the general public is not very familiar with her designs for dance shows and performance.[3] Moreover, both on her website and in the latest catalogue *Sculpting the Senses*, not all her dance or theatre projects are mentioned, which makes the research more difficult. In this chapter I will explore some of van Herpen's designs for dance, opera and theatre in relation to the moving body.

Synergy of Crossovers

Designing costumes for dancers presents a unique set of challenges. Dance companies often include large numbers of performers, meaning that costumes must be produced in higher quantities, which requires different approaches to both design and production. Furthermore, small details and delicate handwork are often lost on audiences viewing the stage from a distance, so the priority in designing costumes must be their visual impact. Above all, dancers must be able to move freely – rolling on the floor, stretching, sweating and performing under physically demanding conditions – therefore comfort and flexibility are essential requirements. Costumes also need to be durable enough to withstand months of repeated performances. For these reasons, designing for dance is fundamentally different from creating a one-off haute couture garment. How did Iris van Herpen deal with those challenges and demands?

In the beginning of her career, Iris van Herpen collaborated quite a lot with the Dutch choreographer Nanine Linning. She has been the artistic director of Scapino Ballet in Rotterdam since 2024, after having worked as a choreographer in Germany for the previous decade. According to Jessica Hemmings, van Herpen and Linning worked together on as many as six projects.[4] This was the period in which van Herpen made more extreme experimental designs, put together under the theme 'Mythology of Fear' in the exhibition *Sculpting the Senses* (2023). It may therefore come as no surprise that in the same period, Iris van Herpen designed rather daring costumes for Nanine Linning's dancers. For the first collaborative project, the choreography *Synthetic Twin* (2009), she developed leather costumes with masks.[5] Nanine Linning recalls that the dancers needed a lot of persuasion to accept the leather costumes as they were quite uncomfortable. The suits were extremely tight, restricting movement and causing the dancers to overheat; in addition, they had to wear masks that made both seeing and breathing more difficult. The dresses that Iris van Herpen designed for the same ballet were very heavy; each weighed seven or eight kilos! It is worth quoting Linning at length because her words show the particular burden and demands that Iris van Herpen's designs placed on the performers and dancers:

> As soon as a dancer turns a pirouette, you get a sort of flying force in the fabric, causing you to quickly fly off the rails. We therefore had to rehearse a lot to adapt to the fabric. The dancers really had to train to be able to jump in these dresses. It took quite a lot of effort. But creating hardcore work is exactly my style. That is the nice thing about Iris: she also works in a very hardcore and radical way. We

keep going and trying when something is impossible; that is what we have in common.[6]

Hardcore indeed; Iris van Herpen may have enjoyed dancing herself in her youth, but she did not spare the dancers when designing challenging experimental costumes for them.

Some of the leather costumes were drawn from the all-leather couture collection 'Mummification' (S/S 2009; see Figure 5.1), created in the same year as the ballet.[7] Inspired by the macabre beauty of ancient Egyptian mummification, Iris van Herpen developed highly labour-intensive couture pieces. Using intricate techniques such as swaddling and wrapping, many of the designs consist of countless leather strips bound together, forming the complex, three-dimensional layers that have become a hallmark of her style. Those leather strips also make up the design for the somewhat eerie costumes and masks for the choreography *Synthetic Twin*.

Also for another collaborative project, the production of Puccini's opera *Madame Butterfly* (2012), Iris van Herpen designed challenging costumes. The lead singer for the main character, Madame Butterfly, could hardly move nor sit in her white expansive costume, while singers had difficulties performing in a corset. Linning says: 'We had to either adjust the choreography or the costumes.' At Linning's request, van Herpen also designed huge, 'extreme', wigs to create Japanese manga looks. In this context, Linning emphasises how much

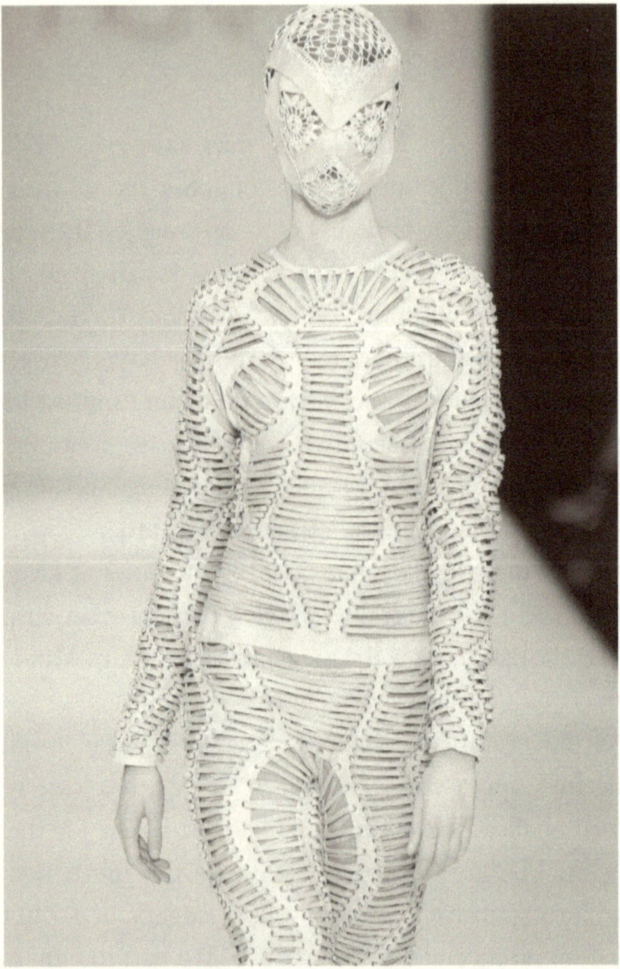

Figure 5.1 Iris van Herpen, collection 'Mummification', S/S 2009. Dress and mask made of beige leather strips, which served as inspiration for the dance costumes of Nanine Linning's choreography *Synthetic Twin*. © Photographer Michel Zoeter.

she loves fashion because of its 'three-dimensionality, sensuality, and tactility. Fashion stimulates the senses!'[8]

Linning obviously enjoys stimulating the senses of the dancers because she invited Iris van Herpen again to design the costumes for the choreography *ZERO* in 2013. Here, the designs were rimmed with spiky transparent triangles like some of the designs for 'Capriole', her debut collection as a member of the Chambre Syndicale de la Haute Couture (A/W 2011). Van Herpen designed the layers of jagged-edge pieces on the computer and produced them in the 3D printer, using acrylic material.[9] The spikes are reminiscent of ice floes and look quite fierce. Indeed, writes Jessica Hemmings, 'The sharp edges of the triangles meant the dancers in *ZERO* risked cutting each other if their movements were too close to each other.'[10]

Van Herpen worked with choreographer Nanine Linning in the early years of her career; years in which her cutting-edge designs were rather edgy, to say the least. No wonder that the costumes challenged dancers (and singers) beyond their comfort zone. In the words of Iris van Herpen herself:

> People who journey to the edge of the imaginable open my awareness to both the possibilities and the limitations of my brain, and give rise to my imagination and creativity. My imagination propels my thoughts faster and further than reality, which is frustrating, but my conviction about what I can make and do in the future obliges me to keep on exploring.[11]

Shimmering

In the next years, Iris van Herpen was highly active in creating more dance costumes, for example for choreographer Benjamin Millepied's ballet *Neverwhere* for the New York City Ballet in 2014, and two years later for his ballet *Clear, Loud, Bright, Forward* for the Opéra de Paris in 2016. The next year she designed the costumes for choreographer Sasha Waltz's ballet *Kreatur*, Berlin in 2017.[12] And in the following year, she designed the costumes for all the singers and dancers in Claude Debussy's opera *Pelléas et Mélisande* for the Opera Vlaanderen in Antwerp in 2018, for which Damien Jalet and Sidi Larbi Cherkaoui did the choreography and Marina Abramović created the set.[13] It is quite fascinating to see how well van Herpen's fantasy costume designs fit into the dreamy worlds of impressionistic or modernist ballet performances.

I cannot discuss them all here, so I concentrate on the costumes that Iris van Herpen designed for the ballet *Neverwhere* for the New York City Ballet in 2014. Choreographer Benjamin Millepied had invited her because he liked the 'incredibly graphic and powerful' quality of her designs.[14] The black costumes were based on her collection 'Hybrid Holism' and made of layered acrylic sheets (see Figure 5.2). Millepied was impressed how the black plastic glittered on the stage: '[…] the way they shimmer and reflect light is amazing', making a lasting visual impact on the audience.[15] The layering enabled the costumes to fold and unfold, but the movement of the plastic

Figure 5.2 Iris van Herpen, collection 'Hybrid Holism', A/W 2012, Look 3. The black dress of layered acrylic sheets served as inspiration for the dance costumes of Benjamin Millepied's ballet *Neverwhere*. © Peter Stigter Team.

sheets made quite a lot of noise. Millepied was most impressed, however, with the *pointe* boots that van Herpen designed for the ballet: 'She had to know *pointe* shoes to understand how to develop those – it's all very technical, so it's definitely a plus that she has that knowledge and also that interest.'[16] It is then van Herpen's embodied knowledge of dance practice that enabled her to create *pointe* boots, by pulling plastic boots over the *pointe* shoes, creating an alien look that she has often produced for her shoes in those years – mostly in cooperation with the company United Nude.[17] The look was so striking that a picture features on the poster for an exhibition on Dance and Fashion at the Fashion Institute of Technology in New York in 2014, as well as for the cover of the ensuing book.[18]

The dance costumes for *Neverwhere* are informed by similar designs that Iris van Herpen created for her collection 'Hybrid Holism' a few years earlier (A/W 2012), although they also resemble a look from an earlier collection 'Escapism' (S/S 2011; see Figure 2.2).[19] This collection was inspired by the architectural, interactive installation 'Hylozoic Ground' by the Canadian architect and artist Philip Beesley, which he made for the Venice Biennale in 2010.[20] Beesley and van Herpen had not yet met, but they did so a year later in 2013 and from then on have sustained a highly productive collaborative practice, crossing and even merging disciplines of fashion and architecture.[21] 'Hylozoic' refers to Hylozoism, the ancient Greek belief that all matter is in some sense alive or animated.[22] Greek 'hyle' means matter, while 'zoē' means life. This idea of course very much speaks to van Herpen's philosophy of life, and she mentions it as the source of inspiration for her collection 'Hybrid Holism'.

This way of thinking refers back to the philosophical perspective of new materialism that I introduced in Chapter 2. Choreographer Millepied was impressed with the shimmering quality of the black acrylic costumes that van Herpen had designed for his ballet. Shimmering refers to the play of natural light, from the surface of water in a pond after it has rained, to the twinkling of the stars in the sky. Philosopher Rosi Braidotti calls this 'the shimmering materiality of the world'.[23] Shimmering expresses the vitality and brilliance of the light, its dynamic dancing quality, for example in the aesthetic qualities of bioluminescence in algae that van Herpen explored in 'the living dress' that I discussed in the previous chapter. For new materialists, this idea of shimmering goes further: shimmering highlights the sensuality and vitality of all matter. It encompasses light, but also all kinds of vibrations in cells and molecules. Shimmering, writes Braidotti, 'manifests a deep enchantment with the world, an engagement with its perennial flows of activity'.[24] Again, this lines up well with Iris van Herpen's design practice. In Chapter 3, I quoted her about vibrations in the human body, but here I will expand the citation from that interview:

> In a lot of my designs, I express the vibrational qualities of our bodies. Every cell inside us is creating energy and vibrations at the atomic level, and our heart produces

> an electromagnetic field. When I look at someone I find it beautiful to imagine how he or she would look at that moment if I could see all of his or her energy, all of that vibration. When I think of all the trillions of vibrations that happen simultaneously inside us, I feel overwhelmed. And it is that overwhelming feeling of wonder and transformation that I want to bring to the other side of the skin, like a micro-dance of movement all around you.[25]

In this poetic and even spiritual quote, Iris van Herpen shows to fully sympathise with the ancient Greek belief of Hylozoism that all matter is alive and animated. This vital materialist view of life is beautifully expressed in the short dance film *Biomimicry* that I will now discuss.

Biomimicry

Biomimicry derives, like so many words or titles that Iris van Herpen uses, from ancient Greek, 'bios' meaning life, and 'mimesis' meaning imitation. It refers to the simulation of life, but in modern times it means more specifically to replicate models, systems and elements of nature for the purpose of solving complex human problems (says Wikipedia). The short dance film *Biomimicry* (2020) obviously does not intend to solve problems of today, but it does show the beauty of the human body as vibrant and intelligent matter, as well as its ability to merge with the environment.[26]

Iris van Herpen made the short film in collaboration with the Dutch National Ballet in 2020, featuring dancer Jingjing Mao, and directed by Ryan McDaniels, while the music was created by Thijs de Vlieger and Lavinia Meijer. The website of the Dutch National Ballet writes the following about the idea for the film:

> The concept of the creation stems from the notion of biomimicry – the design and production of materials and systems that are modelled on biological processes. In line with Iris van Herpen's continuous pursuit to materialise the invisible forces that structure the world, the film focusses on the bond between humanity and nature while showcasing the intersection of both with infinite expansion and contraction.[27]

In order to see how Iris van Herpen visualised biomimicry, let me look at the short, four-minute film and the dresses in more detail. The classical ballet dancer Jingjing Mao wears four different dresses from several collections. The most striking stylistic feature of the dresses for this short dance film is their fluidity, flowing with and along the body of the dancer.

Mao starts her pirouettes and *en pointe* work in a short black and white organza dress from the 'Seijaku' collection (look 7, A/W 2016). The camera at one point concentrates on the three-dimensional folds of plissé fabric around the navel, showing the intricacy as well as the movement of the folds.

For this collection Iris van Herpen tried to visualise sound waves as evolving geometric patterns. The black and white dresses 'float on a 3D moiré technique in which hand-pleated and line-printed organza is handstitched on transparent tulle. The lightest Japanese organza is woven from threads five times thinner than human hair and made with the traditional Shibori technique.'[28] Shibori is a folding technique to create patterns on fabric by binding, wrapping and dyeing. The thin fabric lends itself perfectly for the flowing movement of the dancer. As Iris van Herpen says, 'You always need movement in clothes.'[29]

The dancer then wears a short dress from the collection 'Between the Lines' (look 2, S/S 2017). The look of the dress is both transparent and plastic, but it is surprisingly flexible. For this collection Iris van Herpen focused on patternmaking by building up lines in patterns and then distorting them. To enhance the optical illusion of distortion, she worked with repetitive patterns in white. The new technique included 'soft 3D hand-casted PU fabrics that are hand-painted through injection moulding and fine expandable laser-cut Mylar fabric'.[30] The play of lines that she introduced in this collection has become another staple stylistic feature of her fashion designs in the next years.

From white and almost transparent dresses, the dancer continues in a long flowing and colourful dress in shades of purple and ochre from the collection 'Shift Souls' (look 10, S/S 2019; see Figure 5.3). The new technology for this dress included

Figure 5.3 Dancer Jingjing Mao wears look 10 from Iris van Herpen's collection 'Shift Souls', S/S 2019. The dress is made of translucent organza in ochre and purple colours, with multidimensional prints and voluminous layering. Image from the short film *Biomimicry* for the Dutch National Ballet, 2020. Director: Ryan McDaniels. © Photographer Valentine Bouquet.

a highly complicated printing process that translates clouds of colours in high resolution onto translucent organza, 'to be layered into nebulous multi-dimensional prints'.[31] This is again a dress made of very thin fabric that dances with the body. The dancer then continues to dance in a long vibrant-blue dress, also from the collection 'Shift Souls' (look 1). This voluminous dress is folded and pleated by hand in complicated folds. Iris van Herpen recounts that for this collection she was inspired by 'the imagination and the fluidity within identity change in Japanese mythology'.[32] She was particularly interested in the idealisation and the hybridisation of the female body, so as 'to explore the deeper meaning of identity and how immaterial and mutable it can become'.[33]

Towards the end of the very short film, the editing intermingles the four dresses with the movement of the dancer; she lifts a leg in one dress and finishes the movement in another, turns in another dress and bends in yet another one.

Biomimicry is a fantasy dreamscape where dance and fashion interlace. For this film, van Herpen has moved far away from the heavy leather suits or noisy acrylic dresses of earlier designs for dance shows. On the contrary, here the dresses are all fluffy and flowing, fluid and flexible. The smoothness is enhanced by cinematic means: All movement is shown in slow motion, while the editing creates a seamless continuation between the movement of the female body and the movement of the garments. The soft lighting adds to the dreamy landscape of the desert dunes that are projected in the background. The music combines the woody yet angelic sound of the harp with more machinic tones.

The film shows a world of folds par excellence: the dunes, the body, the garments and the music – everything undulates. This dance is a game of folding, enfolding and unfolding. As we saw in the chapter on the fold, the continuous process of folding and unfolding can be related to the fluidity of identity – and it is interesting to read that Iris van Herpen was particularly interested in the immateriality and mutability of identity when she worked on the collection 'Shift Souls'. In *Biomimicry* the 'liquescent shapes'[34] of the dancer point to the hybridisation of the female body and the exploration of the deeper meaning of identity that Iris van Herpen seeks. The body is in constant flux and the multilayered folds of van Herpen's designs become pure movement that embrace the embodied subject, but from which the body can also free itself. The perpetual motion in the dance film shows the body as incorporeal, a body of passions, affect and intensity.

The desired flexibility can also be attributed to some of the characteristics of classical ballet. The tall and graceful body of the dancer Jingjing Mao seems to defy gravity, as ballet dancers are bound to do, through the lifts of her leg, the jumps in the sky, the pirouettes and of course the *pointe* technique. Those dance techniques together make the female dancer appear weightless and sylph-like – not unlike the quivering organza dresses around her. While there is a suggestion of an ethereal body here, the dancer moves in space and fully takes up its three-dimensionality, again enhanced by the voluminous silhouettes of the dresses. There is thus a double movement of freedom: The folds of fabric are freed from the body, just as the body is freed from the material restrictions of the dresses. Here I repeat a quote from the chapter on folds that explains how van Herpen has introduced fluidity into her designs: 'her dresses come to life with the slightest movement of the body, creating a ballet of textures and materials, friction and shifts, colours and transparency', as curator Cloé Pitiot writes.[35]

Biomimicry claims to visualise 'a future in which mankind, science and nature are closely interwoven'.[36] This is not entirely apparent to me, but as Vanessa Gerrie writes in the context of Iris van Herpen's designs for dance, she does 'manifest not only a hybridised design identity but a hybridised way in which fashion can be perceived, that is, not something to solely be consumed but a unique medium in which to explore the human condition and our relationship with technology and nature'.[37] *Biomimicry* shows the sensitive interface between the body and its environment. By focusing on the movement of body and fabric, van Herpen creates a sensory experience that highlights the importance of the space beyond the body. It is a process of becoming: the dancer becomes a bird, a peacock, a fish. The story of biomimicry that it tells is not for the benefit of an anthropocentric tale. As Iris van Herpen writes about her own ideas on fashion design on her website:

> Through biomimicry I look at the forces behind the forms in nature, these patterns and natural cycles are my guide to explore new forms. I continue to ask, can emotions be materialised? I believe it's possible to merge, stir and sculpt our senses through a sensitive balance of textures, shapes and colors.[38]

Ignoring a narrative, the short film *Biomimicry* rather foregrounds something more elemental and emotional. The telling detail here is a haunting close-up in the film: Jingjing Mao wears a mask, made by Iris van Herpen, which comes from a later collection, 'Sensory Seas' (S/S 2020). The mask is flexible and does not cover the entire face, but it does make the dancer's face alien, perhaps insect-like. She becomes a butterfly, enjoying a process of becoming: leaping into the future, when the future is more than human. As Iris van Herpen says in a different context: 'We will have multiple identities in our near future, and I wanted to create garments that blur our assumptions about what it means to be embodied and what it means to be human.'[39]

In this chapter I have traced van Herpen's development in designing costumes for dancers and other performers. Her artistic designs unfold across multiple materials and spaces, from heavy, leathery or plasticky matter that would stick to the dancers' bodies to flowing organza dresses that put wings on their feet. She exits the stage in a line of flight that explores multiple combinations of our embodied identities in unexpected ways. Bodies, materials and desires flow together, 'becoming-with' the dancer in a collaborative choreography that vibrates and shimmers, opening up the infinite potential of what it means to be human.

Notes

1 Iris van Herpen, *A Magazine Curated by Iris van Herpen*. No. A13. (Antwerp: A Publisher, 2014), 13. https://amagazinecuratedby.com /collection/iris-van-herpen/.

2 Vanessa Gerrie, *Borderless Fashion Practice: Contemporary Fashion in the Metamodern Age.* (New Brunswick: Rutgers University Press, 2023), 134. See also Valerie Steele (ed.), *Dance and Fashion.* (New Haven: Yale University Press, 2014); the cover picture of the book is a ballerina in a design by Iris van Herpen (see also note 18). https://exhibitions.fitnyc.edu/dance-and-fashion/publication/.

3 Jessica Hemmings, 'Iris van Herpen: The Body'. *Textile: Cloth and Culture* 23, nos. 3–4 (2025): 888–901.

4 Ibid.

5 For a short video, see Josanne Buiting, 'Nanine Linning, Synthetic Twins'. YouTube, 2009. https://www.youtube.com/watch?v=OAzuOTzZ0gk.

6 Nanine Linning quoted in Ninke Bloemberg (ed.), *Het Nieuwe Ambacht: Iris van Herpen en haar inspiratie* ['The New Craft: Iris van Herpen and Her Inspiration']. (Utrecht: Centraal Museum, 2011), 36, my translation.

7 The collection 'Mummification' is no longer available on Iris van Herpen's own website. See instead: https://cxainc.com/portfolio/24788/.

8 Nanine Linning in Bloemberg, *Het Nieuwe Ambacht*, 37, my translation.

9 Catalogue *Iris van Herpen: Transforming Fashion.* (Co-published by the High Museum of Art, Atlanta and the Groninger Museum, 2015), n.p.

10 Hemmings, 'Iris van Herpen: The Body', 897.

11 van Herpen, *A Magazine Curated by Iris van Herpen*, 13.

12 https://www.sashawaltz.de/gjbpr7p8fy.

13 https://www.irisvanherpen.com/news/pellas-et-mlisande. See also: https://damienjalet.com/project/pelleas-et-melisande/.

14 Millepied quoted in *A Magazine Curated by Iris van Herpen*, 63.

15 Ibid.

16 Ibid.

17 https://www.irisvanherpen.com/news/iris-van-herpen-x-united-nude-exhibition.

18 A picture of the poster can be found on Iris van Herpen's website: https://www.irisvanherpen.com/news/dance-n-fashion-exhibition-the-museum-at-fit-ny. The book is: Steele, *Dance and Fashion.*

19 https://www.irisvanherpen.com/collections/hybrid-holism.

20 *A Magazine Curated by Iris van Herpen*, 17. See also: https://www.philipbeesleystudioinc.com/sculpture/hylozoic-ground-venice-biennale/.

21 Quoted in Hans Ulrich Obrist, 'Interview with Iris van Herpen' in Catalogue *Iris van Herpen: Sculpting the Senses.* (Amsterdam: Lannoo, 2023), 32.

22 https://www.irisvanherpen.com/collections/hybrid-holism/behind-the-scenes-2.

23 Rosi Braidotti, *Posthuman Feminism.* (Cambridge: Polity Press, 2022), 178.

24 Braidotti, *Posthuman Feminism*, 181.

25 Obrist, 'Interview with Iris van Herpen', 29.

26 https://www.operaballet.nl/en/articles/biomimicry.

27 Ibid.

28 https://www.irisvanherpen.com/collections/seijaku/seijaku-behind-the-scenes-by-molly-sj-lowe.

29 *A Magazine Curated by Iris van Herpen*, 23.

30 https://www.irisvanherpen.com/collections/between-the-lines/between-the-lines-behind-the-scenes-by-molly-sj-lowe.

31 https://www.irisvanherpen.com/collections/shift-souls/shift-souls-photography-by-molly-sj-lowe. See also Anneke Smelik, 'Fractal Folds: The Posthuman Fashion of Iris van Herpen'. *Fashion Theory* 26, no. 1 (2022): 5–26.

32 https://www.irisvanherpen.com/collections/shift-souls/shift-souls-photography-by-molly-sj-lowe.

33 Ibid.

34 https://www.operaballet.nl/en/articles/biomimicry.

35 Cloé Pitiot, in Catalogue *Iris van Herpen: Sculpting the Senses.* (Amsterdam: Lannoo, 2023), 17.

36 Ibid.

37 Gerrie,. *Borderless Fashion Practice*, 124.

38 https://www.irisvanherpen.com/about/the-maison.

39 Quoted in Obrist, 'Interview with Iris van Herpen', 33.

CONCLUSION: A POSTHUMAN STYLE

Since its establishment in 2007, the Maison of Iris van Herpen has fostered an interdisciplinary exchange across nature, art, science, dance and architecture. This ongoing integration of diverse fields is fundamental to the brand's creative approach, which combines traditional craftsmanship with innovative technologies in progressively sophisticated ways.

Widely regarded as one of fashion's most forward-thinking designers, Iris van Herpen has developed a distinctive aesthetic I describe as posthuman. Her pioneering use of 3D printing brought international recognition, yet technological innovation in her work is inseparable from a deep engagement with nature. She translates nature's beauty, chaos and complexity into fluid, diaphanous and textural forms, where water, air and earth become dynamic structures – from liquid flows to crystalline formations. Her designs stage encounters between craft and technology, the organic and the inorganic, and between art, science and nature.

The posthuman aesthetic emerges from hybrid interactions between tradition and innovation, materiality and immateriality, the organic and the inorganic. Van Herpen dresses a body that is both environmentally situated and technologically permeated. Her work moves fluidly between human and non-human realms, reflecting a view of life as dynamic, entangled and inseparable from nature, materials and technologies. Vibrant and alive, her designs foreground this interdependence through the recurring motif of the fold: ripples, waves, twists and pleats that animate matter and time, suggesting life as a continuous transformation. Shaped by her training in dance, the fold also expresses movement itself, as garment and body expand, become and transform together in an ongoing process of metamorphosis.

In this book, I have shown how van Herpen's work generates a distinctly contemporary aesthetic through the convergence of advanced technologies and meticulous handcraft. This dynamic synergy – high-tech innovation fused with artisanal practice – pushes the boundaries of contemporary fashion. Drawing on the frameworks of new materialism and posthumanism, I have argued that her practice negotiates human and non-human forces along a continuum of nature, culture, biology and technology. Nature remains a central source of inspiration, from water and smoke to mycelium and bird flight, spanning microcosmic and macrocosmic scales. This vision informs her commitment to sustainability, exemplified by the 'living dress' composed of 125 million bioluminescent algae, which integrates living systems into fashion and redefines the relationship between garment and life. Her engagement with the body and movement introduces tensions between experimentation and function, visible in both restrictive and expressive garments she designed for dance. More recent designs shift towards lightness and flow, exploring increasingly fluid and flexible identities.

Looking back on twenty years of Maison Iris van Herpen's fashion design, I discern two distinct periods. In the first decade, more or less from 2007 till 2016, the designs are mostly made of hard materials while the sculptural forms are edgy, daring and otherworldly. From 2015 till 2026 the designs become gradually softer, more fluid and flowing and also more glamorous. The change is most visible in the 'Seijaku' collection: The first looks show highly intricate bulging folds, but they are still made of hard materials in the form of plastic and polyamide sheets arranged on a frame. Other looks in the same collection feature the first flowing organza dresses, folding and waving and truly soft.

The development towards greater softness and fluidity can best be traced in the image of the skeleton. The morphology of the skeleton was first used for the aptly called 'skeleton dress' in the first 3D-printed designs (2010/2011, Figures 1.3 and 2.1). Here, the skeleton was white and hard, and worn in front of the body as if to make the invisible bones on the inside visible on the outside. Throughout the years, the skeletal embodiment remained a recurring motif for Iris van Herpen's designs, until today, but the designs consist of softer materials. For example, for 'Sensory Seas' (S/S 2020), 3D laser-cut waves were heat-bonded to black translucent organza: 'Each layer of organza was hand-stitched onto an embroidered skeletal labyrinth, creating a vibrating exoskeleton of weaving waves.'[1] For 'Meta Morphism' (A/W 2022), Iris van Herpen designed a 3D-printed sculptural bodice, 'partially electroplated with silver', that was draped onto white silk creating a much softer look.[2] Undulating lines following, enhancing and shaping the female body have become one of the most recognisable sculptural forms of van Herpen's designs, for example in 'Roots of Rebirth' (S/S 2021), 'Carte Blanche' (S/S 2023) and 'Architectonics' (A/W 2023), but also in the living algae dress of 'Sympoiesis' (2025).

In the past two years, Iris van Herpen has created what she calls 'aerial sculptures', textile installations of silk, tulle, oil paint, inktense chalk, silk paint, cotton thread, as well as stainless steel tube.[3] She first presented her artwork during the fashion show 'Hybrid Show' in Paris (A/W 2024), where she displayed four monumental art installations from which the models emerged to parade the fashion designs. Not incidentally, this show marked her choice to present collections annually in Paris instead of twice a year.

The size of the artworks is impressive; for instance, 'Weightlessness of the Unknown' measures 580 by 450 by 45 cm (Figure C.1). On her website, she writes that she has used classical moulage techniques, in which she sculpts and drapes directly on a body, or in this instance, on a large tulle base.[4] By covering silk fragments in layers of oil paint, she achieves three-dimensionality. She combines techniques that she has used for her fashion designs as well, from hand-pleating to 3D printing. The artworks, some of which were also shown in the exhibition *Sculpting the Senses* in Rotterdam, are as ephemeral and ethereal as some of her fashion designs. The inspiration for the artworks is very much the same as for the fashion – nature – but instilled

Figure C.1 Iris van Herpen working on her art installation 'Weightlessness of the Unknown', 2024. Silk, tulle, oil paint, inktense chalk, silk paint, cotton thread and stainless steel tube. © Photographer Melissa Schriek.

with a sense of freedom and slowness. The artworks represent waves of water, movement in the air, unravelling in time and space.

Iris van Herpen may very well be an embodiment of the Renaissance ideal of a 'homo universalis', or rather a 'femina universalis'; someone who excels in many aspects of life. She is after all a fashion designer who is accomplished in dance and in art, who is a consummate parachute jumper, and who has developed skills in various areas of knowledge by seeking collaboration with scientists, artists, architects and designers.

She consistently pursues innovation and demonstrates an ongoing commitment to advancing her skills in both art and fashion design. Moreover, she is deeply fascinated with the spiritual experience of life. As she says: 'In that light, I have never been interested in fashion, but only in personal style.'[5] For Iris van Herpen, the intangible process of transformation and metamorphosis is the essence of her posthuman art and fashion design.

To finish in her own words: 'The future is not written yet, and it creates hope to know that we can continue to stretch our boundaries and to recreate each other.'[6]

Notes

1 Iris van Herpen, Catalogue *Iris van Herpen: Sculpting the Senses.* (Amsterdam: Lannoo, 2023), 110.
2 Ibid., 109.
3 https://www.irisvanherpen.com/sculpture.
4 Ibid.
5 Quoted in Hans Ulrich Obrist, 'Interview with Iris van Herpen' in *Catalogue Iris van Herpen: Sculpting the Senses.* (Amsterdam: Lannoo, 2023), 29.
6 Ibid.

APPENDIX

Chronological List of Fashion Haute Couture Collections by Iris van Herpen

- Fragile Futurity, 2007
- Chemical Crows, Spring/Summer 2008
- Refinery Smoke, Autumn/Winter 2008
- Mummification, Spring/Summer 2009
- Radiation Invasion, Autumn/Winter 2009
- Synesthesia, Spring/Summer 2010
- Crystallization, Autumn/Winter 2010
- Escapism, Spring/Summer 2011
- Capriole, Autumn/Winter 2011 (debut show in Paris)
- Micro, Spring/Summer 2012
- Hybrid Holism, Autumn/Winter 2012
- Voltage, Spring/Summer 2013
- Wilderness Embodied, Autumn/Winter 2013
- Biopiracy, Spring/Summer 2014
- Quaquaversal, Spring/Summer 2015
- Magnetic Motion, Autumn/Winter 2015
- Lucid, Spring/Summer 2016
- Seijaku, Autumn/Winter 2016
- Between the Lines, Spring/Summer 2017
- Aeriform, Autumn/Winter 2017
- Ludi Naturae, Spring/Summer 2018
- Syntopia, Autumn/Winter 2018
- Shift Souls, Spring/Summer 2019
- Hypnosis, Autumn/Winter 2019
- Sensory Seas, Spring/Summer 2020
- Roots of Rebirth, Spring/Summer 2021

- Earthrise, Autumn/Winter 2021
- Meta Morphism, Autumn/Winter 2022
- Carte Blanche, Spring/Summer 2023
- Architectonics, Autumn/Winter 2023
- Hybrid Show Autumn/Winter 2024 (first show to include art installations)
- Sympoiesis, Autumn/Winter 2025
- Sonic Starquakes, Autumn/Winter 2026

REFERENCES

Alberti, Leon Battista. *On Painting* (*Della pittura*). Translated by John Spencer. New Haven: Yale University Press, 1966 rev. ed. [orig. 1435–6].

Bennett, Jane. *Vibrant Matter: A Political Ecology of Things*. Durham: Duke University Press, 2010.

Blitzkickers. 'Iris van Herpen ~ Syntopia'. YouTube. Video, 05.35, 2018, accessed 17 April 2026, https://www.youtube.com/watch?v=xtGq1zpTDQo.

Bloemberg, Ninke (ed.). *Het Nieuwe Ambacht: Iris van Herpen en haar inspiratie* ['The New Craft: Iris van Herpen and Her Inspiration']. Utrecht: Centraal Museum, 2011.

Bolton, Andrew. *Manus x Machina: Fashion in an Age of Technology*. New York: The Metropolitan Museum of Art, 2016.

Braidotti, Rosi. *The Posthuman*. Cambridge: Polity Press, 2013.

Braidotti, Rosi. *Posthuman Feminism*. Cambridge: Polity Press, 2022.

Bruno, Giuliana. 'Pleats of Matter, Folds of the Soul'. In *Afterimages of Gilles Deleuze's Film Philosophy*, edited by David Rodowick, 213–33. Minneapolis: University of Minnesota Press, 2010.

Buiting, Josanne. 'Nanine Linning, Synthetic Twins'. YouTube. Video, 02.37 min., 2009, accessed 17 April 2026, https://www.youtube.com/watch?v=OAzuOTzZ0gk.

Carlson, Cajsa. 'Iris van Herpen Dress Covered in Glowing Algae is "Cultivated Rather than Constructed"'. *Dezeen Magazine*, 10 July

2025a, accessed 6 April 2026, https://www.dezeen.com/2025/07/10/glowing-algae-dress-iris-van-herpen/.

———. 'Biodesign Adds "a Whole New Range of Possibilities" to Fashion Says Iris van Herpen'. *Dezeen Magazine*, 25 September 2025b, accessed 6 April 2026, https://www.dezeen.com/2025/09/25/biodesign-fashion-iris-van-herpen-interview/.

Chabot, Splinter. Podcast 'Het geheim van Iris van Herpen' [The Secret of Iris van Herpen], four episodes, in Dutch. Rotterdam: Kunsthal, 2025, accessed 17 April 2026, https://www.kunsthal.nl/nl/podcast-het-geheim-van-iris-van-herpen/.

Clark, Hazel. *Slow*. London: Bloomsbury Series 'Fashion in Action', 2026.

Coogler, Ryan. *Film Black Panther: Wakanda Forever.* Los Angeles: Walt Disney Studios Motion Pictures, Marvel Studios, 2022.

Deleuze, Gilles. *The Fold: Leibniz and the Baroque. Translated by Tom Conley.* Minneapolis: University of Minnesota Press, 1993 (1988).

——— and Félix Guattari. *A Thousand Plateaus: Capitalism and Schizophrenia*. Translated by Brian Massumi. Minneapolis: University of Minnesota Press, 1987 (1980).

Gerrie, Vanessa. *Borderless Fashion Practice: Contemporary Fashion in the Metamodern Age*. New Brunswick: Rutgers University Press, 2023.

Haraway, Donna. *Staying with the Trouble: Making Kin in the Chthulucene.* Durham: Duke University Press, 2016.

Hemmings, Jessica. 'Grown Fashion: Animal, Vegetable or Plastic?' *Textile: The Journal of Cloth & Culture* 6, no. 3 (2008): 262–273.

———. 'Iris van Herpen: The Body'. *Textile: Cloth and Culture* 23, nos. 3–4 2025: 888–901.

Hollander, Anne. *Seeing Through Clothes.* London: Penguin, 1988 (1975).

Ingold, Tim. 'Toward an Ecology of Materials'. *Annual Review of Anthropology*, no. 41 (2012): 427–442. https://doi.org/10.1146/annurev-anthro-081309-145920.

Isar, Nicoletta. 'Sympoiesis'. No year, accessed 6 April 2026, https://artsandculturalstudies.ku.dk/research/art-and-earth/environmental-humanities-glossary/sympoiesis/.

Koek, Ariane. 'On the Edge of the Im/Material'. In *Catalogue Iris van Herpen: Sculpting the Senses*, 232–235. Amsterdam: Lannoo, 2023.

Lovelock, James and Lynn Margulis. 'Atmospheric Homeostasis by and for the Biosphere: The Gaia Hypothesis'. *Tellus* 26, nos. 1–2 (1974): 2–10.

Lowery, David. *Film Mother Mary.* Homebird Productions, 2026.

Macel, Christine. 'Foreword'. In *Catalogue Iris van Herpen: Sculpting the Senses*, 11. Amsterdam: Lannoo, 2023.

Marks, Laura U. *The Fold: From Your Body to the Cosmos.* Durham: Duke University Press, 2024.

McDaniels, Ryan. *Biomimicry.* Short film with dancer JingJing Mao. Video, 4.29 min., 2020, accessed 21 April 2026, https://www.youtube.com/watch?v=_BE89JP7Rhc.

McQuillan, Deirdre. 'Visionary Designer Iris Van Herpen Combines Technology with Craftsmanship in Ways Like No Other'. *The Irish Times*, 19 August 2024, accessed 6 April 2026, https://www

.irishtimes.com/life-style/fashion/2024/08/19/visionary-designer-iris-van-herpen-combines-technology-with-craftsmanship-in-ways-like-no-other/.

Moore, Kellina. 'Designing for a Pop Star'. *The New York Times*, 17 April 2026, accessed 22 April 2026, https://www.nytimes.com/2026/04/17/style/mother-mary-costumes-iris-van-herpen.html?smid=url-share.

Myers, William. *Bio Design: Nature, Science, Creativity*. 3rd edn. London: Thames and Hudson, 2022 (2012).

Obrist, Hans Ulrich. 'Interview with Iris van Herpen'. In *Catalogue Iris van Herpen: Sculpting the Senses*, 24–33. Amsterdam: Lannoo, 2023.

Quinn, Bradley. *Textile Futures. Fashion, Design and Technology*. Oxford: Berg, 2010.

———. *Fashion Futures*. London: Merrell, 2012.

Rocamora, Agnès and Anneke Smelik. 'Introduction'. In *Thinking Through Fashion: A Guide to Key Theorists*, 2nd edn, edited by Agnès Rocamora and Anneke Smelik, 1–26. London: Bloomsbury, 2025.

SHOWstudio. 'Watch Iris Van Herpen's Syntopia Couture Collection Come to Life'. YouTube. Video, 02:22, 2018, accessed 6 April 2026, https://www.youtube.com/watch?v=GSTRyPWRJpw.

Smelik, Anneke. 'Fashioning the Fold: Multiple Becomings'. In *The Deleuzian Century: Art, Activism, Society*, edited by Rosi Braidotti and Rick Dolphijn, 37–55. Amsterdam: Brill Rodopi, 2014.

———. 'Cybercouture: The Fashionable Technology of Pauline van Dongen, Iris van Herpen and Bart Hess'. In *Delft Blue to Denim*

Blue. Contemporary Dutch Fashion, edited by Anneke Smelik, 252–69. London: I.B. Tauris/Bloomsbury, 2017.

———. 'New Materialism: A Theoretical Framework for Fashion in the Age of Technological Innovation'. *International Journal of Fashion Studies*, 5, no. 1 (2018): 33–54. https://doi.org/10.1386/infs.5.1.33_1.

———. 'A Posthuman Turn in Fashion'. In *Routledge Companion to Fashion Studies*, edited by Veronica Manlow, Eugenia Paulicelli and Elizabeth Wissinger, 57–64. New York: Routledge, 2021.

———. 'Fractal Folds: The Posthuman Fashion of Iris van Herpen'. *Fashion Theory* 26, no. 1 (2022): 5–26. https://doi.org/10.1080/1362704X.2020.1850035.

———. 'A Dance of Materials: Between the Organic and Inorganic in Iris van Herpen's Fashion'. *National Gallery of Victoria Art Journal*, Australia, 11 December 2023. https://www.ngv.vic.gov.au/essay/a-dance-of-materials-between-the-organic-and-inorganic-in-iris-van-herpens-fashion/.

———. 'Exhibition Review of "Iris van Herpen: Sculpting the Senses"'. *Critical Studies in Fashion & Beauty* 15, no. 2 (2024): 245–249. https://doi.org/10.1386/csfb_00080_5.

———. 'Gilles Deleuze: Bodies-without-Organs in the Folds of Fashion'. In *Thinking through Fashion. A Guide to Key Theorists*, 2nd edn, edited by Agnès Rocamora and Anneke Smelik, 175–88. London: Bloomsbury, 2025.

Spinney, Laura. 'Science on the Catwalk: Iris van Herpen Gives Gowns a Glow Up'. *Nature*, 8 July 2025, accessed 6 April 2026, https://www.nature.com/immersive/d41586-025-02068-x/index.html.

Steele, Valerie. 'A Museum of Fashion Is More Than a Clothes-Bag'. *Fashion Theory* 2, no. 4 (1998): 327–335. https://doi.org/10.2752/136270498779476109.

Steele, Valerie (ed.). *Dance and Fashion*. New Haven: Yale University Press, 2014.

Van Herpen, Iris. *A Magazine Curated by Iris van Herpen*. No. A13. Antwerp: A Publisher, 2014, accessed 17 April 2026, https://amagazinecuratedby.com/collection/iris-van-herpen/.

Verner, Amy. 'It's Alive! Iris Van Herpen's Latest Innovation? A Dress Made From 125 Million Bioluminescent Algae'. *Vogue*, 6 July 2025, accessed 6 April 2026, https://www.vogue.com/article/iris-van-herpen-living-dress-125-million-bioluminescent-algae.

Catalogues on Iris van Herpen:

- Catalogue for exhibition *Iris van Herpen*. Curators Mark Wilson and Sue-an van der Zijpp. Groningen: Groninger Museum and BAI Publishers, 2012.
- Catalogue for exhibition *Iris van Herpen: Transforming Fashion*. The catalogue was co-published by the High Museum of Art, Atlanta and the Groninger Museum. Curators Sarah Schleuning, High Museum of Art, and Mark Wilson and Sue-an van der Zijpp, Groninger Museum, 2015.
- Catalogue for exhibition *Iris van Herpen*: *Sculpting the Senses*. Curators Cloé Pitiot and Louise Curtis. Musée des Arts Décoratifs in Paris. Amsterdam: Lannoo, 2023.

Websites on Iris van Herpen:

- Website of Maison Iris van Herpen: https://www.irisvanherpen.com/.
- Creative Exchange Agency: https://cxainc.com/artist/iris-van-herpen/.
- Orient Palms has descriptions and pictures of most Couture and Ready-to-wear collections: https://www.orientpalms.com/iris-van-herpen.

INDEX

www.ingramcontent.com/pod-product-compliance
Lightning Source LLC
LaVergne TN
LVHW090508261026
851038LV00037B/355
9781801361170